Hope
Inspires
Strength

Hope Inspires Strength

HOW ONE WOMAN OVERCAME INSURMOUNTABLE ODDS

LIANE K. CHONG

Editorial work and production management by Eschler Editing
Cover design by MiblArt
Interior print design and layout by Sydnee Hyer
eBook design and layout by Sydnee Hyer

Published by Hope to Inspire Publishing

Production services facilitated by Scrivener Books

ISBN: 978-1-949165-21-0

To Dad, who taught and raised me to be the strong person I am today. It's been over sixteen years since he passed away, but the values and lessons he instilled in me have not been and will never be forgotten.

This book is to continue his legacy and fulfill the dream he had of writing a book.

To Mom, my mighty but unsung hero. Her strength and rock-solid attitude went unnoticed until she had to face a physical disability that left her incapacitated and fighting for her life on a couple of occasions. I have learned much from her about attitude, appreciation for life, and flexibility. She inspires many with her perseverance and desire to live.

To Jason, who met me when life was simple and stayed with me through the tough times. He has been a solid foundation for my family and a good husband and father to our children.

To Leah for being such a caring, loving, and compassionate daughter who has always helped to support and take care of her family.

And to Jett, for teaching me unconditional love and happiness. His innocence and purity brings peace and serenity to my life. He is a blessing.

Table of Contents

Acknowledgments

My deepest gratitude goes to my husband, Jason, for encouraging me to share my story. You lived it with me, and as with all my countless, endless projects, you allowed me to pursue it until the dream became a reality.

I would like to thank Dr. Kristie Overstreet, who walked into my life when I decided I would write my book and made sure it came to fruition. The dedication of her time, knowledge, and encouragement is something I can never repay. This book would not be possible without her coaching.

I would also like to thank Jason and my editors, Heidi Brockbank and Michele Preisendorf, for your guidance in pulling this story together.

CHAPTER 1

Lookout Life, Here I Come

I lay in the delivery room in a daze. Only a short while ago, I had been in the agony of a labor so brutal and intense, my blood pressure had risen to dangerously high levels. The child I had longed for, through a miscarriage and failed pregnancy attempts was finally here, only to be whisked away for tests. I knew something was not right, especially as the minutes passed with no word.

When they finally laid my son in my arms, my fears were confirmed. He was so swollen he would eventually lose an inch from his birth measurement. While it would take months to reveal the full extent of Jett's condition, it was heartbreakingly clear that he faced a long, hard road of challenges due to chromosome abnormalities that would come to include cortical blindness, hypotonia, cerebral palsy, autism, and an inability to walk and talk.

That day in late January 2012, I was confused, blindsided, puzzled, and devastated. I wondered why God had given this child to me. Why, on top of all the other things I was dealing with, was I given this special child? In some ways, I already felt I had gone nine rounds with life, from losing my father at the age of twenty-seven just six months after getting married and starting my new career, to struggling to establish a career in a nontraditional field for women, to spending the last four years taking care of my mom, who was (and still is) completely bedridden and unable to do anything herself. As a mother of an active five-year-old, full-time businesswoman, and caretaker of my mother, I had such a full plate and it was hard to imagine how I could possibly handle anything else, let alone something of this life-changing magnitude.

In the process of realizing the cards I'd been dealt, I kept coming back to the age-old question we all ask in our lives, sooner or later: Why me? Why was my life so difficult? Why was I chosen to be the mother of my son, and what caused him to be born that way? How come every time I overcame one challenge, life tossed another in my path? In searching for answers, I realized there were no definite or easy answers.

With everything that has happened, there's never been a cut-and-dried explanation. One thing I learned was that while I could never be in control of the challenges life gave me or how often they came, I was in control of how I let them define my life and my actions. Though it would be a journey of months and years to come to peace with this new challenge, a seed of hope was planted in my heart that day. Somehow, I would survive *and thrive*, even though in that moment, I had no idea what that future looked like.

In the days to come, I looked deep inside myself for strength. I needed it daily, some days a lot more than others. I knew I had to focus on the positive and rely on hope to understand that what I was dealing with at the time could only get better. And if it didn't or couldn't get better, I had to convince myself I could learn to accept and deal with it better in time.

One thing that gave me hope in those dark moments was a growing feeling that I might be able to use my struggles as a way to help others in theirs. The more I thought about that, the more right it felt. There was a strange sense of peace when I considered my situation through that lens. How else could I explain the challenges life had presented me with? If I could live a successful life as a wife, mother, business owner, and daughter and thrive during the process, I could share how I did it. I could provide inspiration, motivation, and strength to help people find the hope they needed for their lives. I could help demonstrate how life could change in an instant and how you could successfully tackle anything thrown your way. I could do it leading by example. I could give hope and insight to help other people realize that no matter how hard your life is, someone is dealing with something harder and that you can get through anything and still love yourself and be grateful for your life and the blessings in it.

We are blessed with this amazing thing called life, each of us with our own unique journey. Your life can seem terrific—until tragedy strikes. Or you can feel like your life is hopeless and then it turns around for the better. My life has been an eventful journey with many ups and downs. I've experienced career setbacks, losing loved ones, being a caretaker for chronically ill parents, and having a child with special needs. Each struggle has brought its own heartbreak. Yet no matter what has come my way, I have been able to stay positive—because of hope. When my world seems relentless and unforgiving, I can always hope things will get better, and I allow myself to believe that. It's truly amazing how strong you can be and the things you can persevere through with the right attitude and with hope. I want to share how hope has helped me in my journey and can also help you with whatever comes your way.

I hope you will join me as I share my experiences with not only heartache, fears, doubt and discouragement but courage, perseverance, heart, and hope. Come and look back at the turmoil I have experienced over the last seventeen years. I want to share what I've learned on my journey. I want you to know that you can get through anything life throws at you. I want you to know you are never alone, even in your darkest hours. And I want you to know you can still find peace, hope, and joy (and even laughter) no matter how bad things get.

My Foundation

"A self-made man who came from humble beginnings"—that was how my grandfather described my dad in his funeral dedication video. Even though I grew up in an affluent family, I never wanted to be called a spoiled brat. I wanted to be a good child and make my parents proud. I wanted to do the right thing, to stay out of trouble, and to have a simple, happy life. My parents did a good job of helping me achieve that. I understood the sacrifices they made and knew their childhoods had been so much more difficult than mine. I will be forever grateful for the financial foundation they provided, the stable home environment, and the strong mental toughness I witnessed growing up in Honolulu, Hawaii.

My father was raised in Kalihi, Hawaii, the oldest of three children. While his family was very poor and he didn't have a lot of things while growing up, he was determined to be the best at everything he did. He was a star athlete who played football in high school and at the University of Hawaii at Manoa. He was a bodyguard for a former governor in Hawaii and also acted on a famous local television show in the 1980s. He became an aikido master who trained in and taught martial arts for many

years. It was through this training and his natural gift of healing that he created a specialized form of massage. He also manufactured his own line of vitamin supplements. With his unique massage technique and the right combination of vitamin supplements, he was able to improve the health and well-being of many clients over the thirty-plus years he was in business.

Mom and Dad at Dad's 41st Yakudoshi birthday party

My mother was also the eldest of three children and grew up in Kaimuki, Hawaii, attending public school and then also the University of Hawaii at Manoa. Mom also had a hard life. At the age of fourteen, she was severely injured while riding in the back of a station wagon that was rear-ended. She was paralyzed and stayed in the hospital for two weeks before recovering. That same year, her mother had a stroke and passed away. The years that followed brought with them much turmoil at home, and she went to live with another family. She never shared all the details, but I know that following the death of her mother, Mom faced a lot of adversity.

Knowing some of the struggles my parents went through growing up made me realize how simple and good my life was. Dad was my safety net. He always made sure we were taken care of. My mom was our stability. Nothing ever really changed with her. She was always there, always reliable. I felt protected, loved, and grounded and had a deep appreciation for the life they provided me and the sacrifices they made. One day after college, I told my dad, "Thank you for paying for my college. I know it was expensive and appreciate you working so hard to pay for it."

My brother and I are close in age and were close growing up, despite our different activities. Each of my parents had a brother and sister, but challenges like distance, death, and disability prohibited my aunts and uncles from being a big part of my life, though there was one aunty who was active in my life and one set of grandparents who helped raise us. Happily, the employees and apprentices who worked for my father were an extension of my family, and so I never felt lonely or deprived—although having people around and things to do was contingent on my dad being alive.

My husband comes from a large, close-knit family that enjoys many gatherings and activities. Being a part of their family is good because the void left by my dad's passing was filled with new things to do and new places to go. It has been a blessing to be included and to have a lot of support from Jason's family.

I am beyond grateful for the support of his family (his parents, grandparents, aunties and uncles, and three siblings) over the last seventeen years. However, I often wish I had more siblings, that Dad was still alive, and that Mom was physically capable of helping me, especially on the days I'm so exhausted my emotional cup overflows and I find myself in tears.

Over the years, Mom has reminded me I shouldn't let things get me too down because I cannot change my situation. Our foundation, which I refer to as my family, changes as time passes. The way our life looks when we come into this world is vastly different when we leave it. It's important to always remember what we've learned from those who came before us and to continue their legacy for those who follow after us. Whatever happens in between, it's important to keep the foundation solid. When our foundation cracks or starts to fall apart, we need to fight to keep it together for ourselves and those we care about.

Finding Work After College

"She got a job offer for $35,000 to work at this major company." "He got an offer to work at this huge company starting at $33,000 a year." "She has had several interviews with large firms." I was hearing these things about my college classmates, but it was crickets for me. As my days at the University of Puget Sound were coming to an end in May of 1998, I had no clue what I was going to do with my business-management degree. I knew I wasn't the only one who was graduating without a job offer or didn't know what I was going to do after college, but it sure felt that way.

Since I had minored in Japanese, I applied for the JET program to teach English in Japan for a year. I thought I was a perfect candidate, but to my surprise, I wasn't accepted. Though I felt discouraged and embarrassed, I figured it was not meant to be.

When I moved to Hawaii the summer after college, I realized that there's a reason for everything. Not getting into the program ended up being a positive. My parents went through a rough patch in their marriage and needed my support. I also started dating Jason that summer. This was the first time I realized it's important to trust that God has a greater plan and that you cannot force things.

I went back home after graduating to look for work. Although I worked a variety of jobs each break and between semesters, they were temporary and not the kind of jobs that prepared you for a career. I needed to make a decent living and didn't want to feel like money was wasted on my education. I told myself I would build my career in baby steps.

I turned to the classifieds, where I found an ad for data entry and HR, which turned out to be an internal administrative-assistant position at a staffing agency. The job sounded interesting, but I had no office experience. I couldn't even type that fast. I was excited to get a "real job" and had a positive attitude which must have been contagious, because they hired me. Although the job was very fast paced and challenging, I excelled at it beyond the owner's expectations.

Jason had attended college in the Midwest with many of my high school friends. We met during the winter break of our senior year of college and stayed in touch over the last semester. After graduating, we both came back to Hawaii and started dating before he moved to Oregon for additional schooling. We had gotten serious over the summer and continued a long-distance relationship during the fall. Knowing Jason would be in Oregon for three to four more years, I decided to move to Oregon in January of 1999.

Back then, I was a fitness fanatic. I was on the collegiate dance team, took aerobics every semester, played intramural basketball, lifted weights daily, and also danced hula and Tahitian in the annual spring luau. I loved the variety of activities, as anything that required coordination came naturally to me. When I first moved to Portland, Oregon, I was hopeful I would get a job selling memberships at a large national gym. It was a couple of months before I finally got an interview, but the company didn't want me. I remember feeling discriminated against because I was a female and most of the salespeople were men.

What was I going to do for three years while Jason finished school? After a number of fruitless interviews, I considered selling disability insurance to self-employed people in the blue-collar industry. Once I realized what the job actually entailed—driving around town looking for plumbers, electricians, and other vehicles parked alongside the road or in the driveways of homes and approaching them to sell policies—and how dangerous that was for a twenty-two-year-old female, I took a temp-to-hire job as a marketing-department administrator for a few months. I declined the full-time position because I was bored. I had a low threshold for the mundane and constantly needed to be challenged.

Since my first real full-time job was with the staffing agency in Hawaii, I considered staying in that field. As luck would have it, just as my marketing-admin position was ending, a job at the parent company of the staffing service I worked for in Hawaii opened up. The parent company's small office in Portland was nothing like their highly successful office in Hawaii, but I saw an opportunity to grow the branch. I took the job and helped build the branch by placing job ads, interviewing, sending people on jobs, processing payroll, and marketing candidates to employers.

After several months of office work, an opportunity to do outside sales came about. Because I thought it was the only job that would allow me to earn money based on my performance, I convinced the office to promote me. I was still new to Portland and didn't quite know my way around the city, but I wasn't afraid. There was no Google Maps back then, all I had was a paper roadmap. Fearless, I mapped out the territories I would hit each day. I wasn't confident in my ability to sell, but I was confident in my work ethic. I was persistent and resilient because I didn't complain, make excuses, grumble, or give up easily. And that work ethic paid off. With new business growth from my additional sales, our branch won many awards over the next couple of years.

There were over one hundred staffing agencies in Portland at the time. We did not have a lot of existing accounts, and I needed to find new ones. I loved the challenge of finding ways to get my foot in the door with new clients, and I learned I'm a creative person who thinks outside the box and can take an idea and improve on it. Working for the branch and helping it grow was very fulfilling.

Though I had multiple job offers while I lived in Portland after I had settled into my job at the staffing agency, I decided that money wasn't everything. It was more important to get the right experience and be in a position where I had many responsibilities and could maximize my potential. In addition, I wanted to stay loyal to the company that had taken a chance on me.

When you think about the stages of your life, you realize that change is not only inevitable but constant. You cannot stay at the same level forever. Allowing yourself to grow and take that next step leads to opportunities. Most of the time, opportunities do not come out of nowhere. You must work to create them. Don't be afraid of failing or of what others might think. Believe you can do it.

Moving Back to Hawaii and Getting Married

"Where should I settle down and start my life?" It's the big question every college graduate must ask themselves. Do I follow opportunity, or do I go home and look for opportunity there? For those who live in Hawaii, it's a tough choice to be far away from family. It's not as simple as jumping in a car or taking a two-hour plane ride to visit loved ones. The Pacific Ocean makes it all a bit trickier.

We moved back to Hawaii in April 2002. This time I was blessed to move home with a job because the owner of a local CPA firm and payroll company had paid a staffing-agency headhunter to find me. We'd spent most of our savings on our move and couldn't afford to buy a place, so we moved into the bottom floor of my parents' house and paid them rent each month. The timing was good because within a year of our moving home, my father had a near-death experience stemming from heart troubles.

In 1995, my parents took a trip to Europe where Dad began experiencing heart issues. When he came back, he was diagnosed with congestive heart failure. He was five feet, nine inches tall and weighed 430 pounds. His heart was double the size of a normal heart and was functioning at only 15 to 20 percent. He was built like a sumo wrestler and had even done a sumo commercial for a car company. Instead of undergoing surgery or doing the treatment the doctor recommended, Dad decided he would cure himself. He thought he could make his heart better by losing weight. One year later, he lost two hundred pounds by hardly eating, taking vitamins, and taking water pills to drain excess water. He spent the next few years toning up and trying to maintain his weight loss. We thought he was getting better.

But in January of 2003, while at a beach house at Sunset Beach, Dad lost consciousness while in the bathroom. Mom called the ambulance, and he was transported to the nearest hospital. We all freaked out because we nearly lost him. It was our first wake-up call. We weren't exactly sure what had caused him to pass out. He was in a coma and completely unresponsive, but his feet would twitch every so often.

Thankfully, after six days, he woke up and was coherent. A couple of days later, he was released and went home. After this incident, Dad had to stay home for a few months to recover and regain his strength. I'm sure it was tough financially, not having any income since he was self-employed.

The weekend before the wedding in July 2003, Dad was hospitalized for blood in his stool. I couldn't believe he was back in the hospital only a few months after his near-death experience. I was afraid he wouldn't be able to walk me down the aisle because he was so fragile, but he told me he would be fine and would be there on my wedding day. Because his mind was so strong, I believed he could overcome anything. Thankfully, he was released from the hospital, and like a champ, was able to walk me down the aisle.

A week after getting married, Jason and I flew to Maui for our honeymoon. While there, I got the dreaded call that my grandma had passed away. This was the grandma who tended to me and my brother and who'd been very active in our lives. Earlier that year, she had been diagnosed with cancer and experienced a mild stroke. My grandma was very pretty and always took good care of herself, but following her stroke, she looked so different she was barely recognizable on the day of my wedding. She had fought hard to hold on so she could celebrate my special day with me, yet I feared her life was coming to an end. One week later she was gone.

My husband, mom, and dad at our wedding in 2003

Despite these setbacks, it seemed things were falling into place. Although I had a job upon moving home and got married, I was only in my midtwenties and wasn't ready for my family to start falling ill. I was glad I had moved home from the mainland and was around for the last couple of years of my dad's and grandmother's lives. Until someone we love has a major medical scare, we don't often realize how fleeting life and the precious moments we have together are. We can't turn back time once our loved ones are gone.

Starting a New Career

I was proud of the fact that Dad had his business for thirty-plus years and Mom had worked for the same hotel corporation just as long. However, staying with one company your entire career is rare. Though I knew I wouldn't be so lucky as to stay with one company forever, I was still looking for stability and a career that allowed me to be in control. I wanted to be self-employed and consequently considered careers in mortgage, real estate, insurance, and financial advising. I had always wanted to be a financial advisor because my parents didn't have a financial plan. From the time I was in high school, I had a strong desire to make sure my family was protected and thought I could help them if I knew what to do.

While in Oregon, I attended chamber of commerce meetings, where I met someone from a financial-advising company. Thinking I might be a good fit for the company, I went to the office and took their personality test. My scores were so low I didn't get an interview. Ironically, that same firm is the firm I work at now.

After four years of outside-sales experience, I interviewed with a couple of people in the financial-services industry back in Hawaii. They were so critical of their candidates they told me my eyebrows were crooked, I didn't have enough wealth, I didn't know enough wealthy people, I didn't have a market, I would work very long hours, and I would fail. I wasn't offended because I knew it was a test of my commitment and desire to succeed in a challenging field. I did temporarily question whether I was good enough or if I needed to come from a wealthy and well-connected family to succeed, but I didn't dwell on it. However, I decided not to pursue advising at the time as my self-confidence was not strong enough. Instead, I chose insurance sales because I thought the two fields were closely related. If I learned to sell insurance and built a solid book, my eventual transition to financial advisor would be smoother later.

A month or two before my wedding, I went to work for someone in insurance. Before I could start selling, I needed to pass four exams and get my life and health licenses. I was told that to pass the tests, I had to take a two-day class where they showed you slides with bullet points on what the exam would cover. You couldn't take any notes, but if you scheduled the test the morning after the class, you would pass. I couldn't believe people actually passed the exams that way, but I had no choice. Thankfully, I passed two of the four sections after the first try. I passed the third the second time.

Because I was working and didn't want to take extra time off to keep attending the class and I had no book to study, I went back three more times to take the fourth section of the test and simply guessed at the answers. I finally got fed up and started researching where I could find a book. Once I found a book, passing was easy because I had something to study. I could have easily given up and said this was a bad sign and I shouldn't do it. But once I decided to do something, I didn't let obstacles get in the way.

I started in the insurance business because I met a general agent who promised to train me, give me leads, and potentially have me take over for him when he retired. Unfortunately, these were all false promises. The one thing he did do was introduce me to a large supplemental-insurance company. With my four years of outside-sales experience, I was used to prospecting employers to introduce a product or service. So instead of sitting there begging to be given business, I went to the company's sales school for training and ran with it. I quit my payroll sales job in October 2003.

The insurance job was commission only, with no base pay, no stipend, and no benefits. I just turned twenty-seven. Jason and I were still living with my parents and paying them rent because in Hawaii, it's common for younger adults to move in with their parents to avoid paying rent and save for a place of their own. It's also common, especially in some cultures, to have multiple generations of family living together and taking care of one another. My childhood home was large and could accommodate multiple people. It was also in a nice neighborhood in a convenient part of town. I loved it and didn't want to move out until we were financially ready. Having just gotten married, we didn't have enough saved for a down payment. Although it was scary to start a commission-only job, I thought it was the best time since our expenses were minimal and we didn't have children yet.

I started in late October because my district sales coordinator had employer groups he needed help enrolling. However, he was so busy he didn't have time to train me. He simply told me to sit and talk to people all day long for two weeks and that he would be in the conference room next door if I had any questions. It's amazing I got through the enrollment and kept going, considering how many mistakes I made. All of it taught me I was pretty good at letting things roll off my back and not losing confidence if things didn't go well. I did not hold on to negative things, I believed failure was not permanent, and I always looked forward and not backward. I took all the mistakes I made as good training and moved on. The year quickly came to an end, and when 2004 started, there were no immediate enrollments; however, I'd been prospecting to secure my own accounts since day one, and some had started to roll in during the first quarter.

At the end of January, the national supplemental-insurance company held their local annual kick-off, where people who earned the different awards you could qualify for in your first two years, as well as other awards given by the state, were recognized. I sat there feeling irritated as I watched people being called up to the stage. I should have been up there. I had no clue what those awards were for, and I hadn't qualified for them because I had started working months after I submitted my contract.

Immediately after, I reached out to my regional manager to learn more about the awards. The next deadline was for the company headquarters' awards trip. Despite being so far away from qualifying, I told him I would qualify for it. Looking back, I don't think I even knew what I was talking about, but I was eager to prove myself and more competitive than I realized. With that drive, I started to accomplish things that surprised even me.

What makes someone successful in sales? It's not always what you would think. As an introvert, I tended to shy away from fast-talking people and certainly didn't think I would be good at sales. However, I was a hard worker with an extremely strong work ethic. I got the highest praise from every employer I worked for, earned financial bonuses, and was always offered a job to go back to when I left. I always looked for ways to do things faster, smarter, and more efficiently than the next person. I didn't think it would be fair to get paid the same salary as someone else if I performed better. I chose sales because you could be paid more than a flat salary and potentially make a lot of money. I knew that in order to be successful at it, I needed to find a product or service I was passionate about.

There was a lot to learn when I first started selling staffing services, payroll, and then insurance, so I read everything I could get my hands on. From sales books to self-help books and everything in between, reading helped me get through the tough times when I doubted my worth. Books inspired me, kept me motivated, and helped me think positive thoughts. There were a couple of authors in particular who had written motivational business books that inspired me. I couldn't wait to prove my worth to the people who had doubted and underestimated me.

What you think about and focus on, whether positive or negative, impacts your thoughts and, more importantly, your beliefs in yourself. Filling my mind with new skills, lessons from successful people, and inspirational stories was priceless.

Have you ever wanted to try something new or better your skill set? Don't wait! You can live your life to the fullest when you make it a point to better yourself each and every day. Read to enrich your knowledge and to stimulate your brain. Take classes that can help you further your career or better your skill set in your profession. Change careers and have the courage to do something you weren't sure you could succeed in doing. We encourage and expect children to learn and get smarter each year in school. As adults, are we doing the same? Don't be afraid to take risks and make changes in your life if it's for the better. Going from working for someone to working for myself was a big risk, but I haven't looked back and was glad I had the courage to take that first step.

CHAPTER 2

A Joy for Every Sorrow

Tragedy Strikes

Why is it that we can predict with relative surety when a new child is going to come in this world but we can rarely predict when we will leave it? And is there an ideal way to leave this earth? Are there things we can do while living to help the people we leave behind? As death is inevitable for all, I find it interesting that a lot of people don't want to think about preparing for the day they leave this earth.

It was the start of a new work week, and although it was President's Day, I still got up early to go to the gym as I normally did. But that morning was different. It was a good thing I was still home when I heard Mom scream for me to come to their bathroom. Something was not right. I could feel it. I raced upstairs to my parents' bathroom and found Dad lying awkwardly between the toilet and bidet. He was unresponsive. I was panicking, but I had no time to spare. Since Jason had a medical background, I ran downstairs and woke him to help me administer CPR, which we did until the fire and ambulance crews arrived. But his heart had stopped. I hoped the paramedics would be able to revive him, yet, despite their best efforts, the ambulance ride to the hospital was a solemn experience.

I never thought Dad would die so soon. He was stronger than that. My world had been turned upside down. I had lost the one person who brought me strength, comfort, and safety. I was young. I'd been married only six months and was just starting my career. I didn't even have kids yet. How could my kids be born into a world where they never got to meet their grandfather? How unfair was that, not only to me, but to them? I was devastated.

How could his life be cut short when he'd been unwilling to die? We knew his previous heart issues had caused other complications—something I'd learned as I attended doctor visits with him prior to his death. However, Dad had convinced himself and everyone around him that he would not die because his mind could conquer his body. How I wished that had been the case, but, as I learned from his passing, the body ultimately wins over the mind. When faced with medical conditions, we can hope that things will get better, but we can't ignore what's actually happening with our body. Ignoring it only limits our ability to make the most of what is.

I took two weeks off to prepare for the funeral and take care of some urgent things. It was fortunate Jason and I lived with my parents and could be there to help Mom with whatever she needed. To be strong for her, I did what I normally do to avoid feeling depressed and sad—I kept busy so that I didn't have time to feel sad or sorry for myself.

In the months that followed, we went through my dad's things, settled his unfinished business, assessed which of his belongings to keep, rented a dumpster a couple of times, and had three garage sales in an attempt to sell his clothing and miscellaneous things before donating them. It was a lot of work. Since we stayed in the house after his passing, we had time to organize everything. We kept a lot of the things he collected or that were valuable to him, but at the end of the day, I wished we'd written or recorded more of his teachings and thoughts. What I do remember of what he taught and instilled in me, I will cherish forever.

Something as traumatic as losing a parent can change the trajectory of your life. While my world was turned upside down after losing my dad, I had just started a new career and committed to myself just two weeks prior to earn all the awards my company offered. So instead of dwelling on my sorrow, I determined not to let his loss negatively impact my life and kept working when I wasn't assisting with family matters.

I ended up qualifying for the Headquarters Award trip and every award offered after it for the first two years. In addition, I won the most awards at the local state kickoff meetings for my 2004 and 2005 performance as a producer and manager. Everything had worked against me until that point, from failing the exam multiple times, to my rough start from lack of training, to losing my father—all within a six-month period. But I chose not to make excuses or allow circumstances beyond my control impact my success. Instead, I focused on taking care of my family and making my father proud.

After Dad passed, one of my biggest concerns was what to do with my childhood home. None of us wanted to leave. Since my dad was the primary payor of the mortgage loan, Mom tried to refinance several times after his passing but didn't make enough to qualify for the loan on her own. Jason had worked as a massage therapist from the time we moved home in 2002, and he was put on the first loan refinance because he had worked longer in one position than I had. We had to refinance a couple more times for different reasons—all of which could have been avoided had my dad purchased life insurance.

Why he had no life insurance, I'll never know, but I suspect a couple of things. One, he couldn't get a good rate because of his height and weight, and two, he thought it was a waste of money because he didn't think he would die young. However, without life insurance, Mom couldn't pay off the mortgage or afford the monthly payments.

Jason and I helped her with the majority of the mortgage while she paid the utilities and her other bills. We instantly went from paying a $500 monthly courtesy rent to thousands of dollars a month. And as the mortgage amount went up over the years with different loans, so did our contributions.

When a spouse passes away and there's no life insurance to help cover future income or pay off a mortgage, it can leave their survivors in a hard place. The last thing someone wants is to lose their spouse and be forced to move as well. Luckily, we didn't have to move because Jason and I were there to help, but it really delayed our life and our ability to save up for a home of our own.

With Dad's death and the start of a new career, 2004 was a tough year. We all have different coping methods. Mine are keeping busy and analyzing my thoughts in the moment—although every so often I have to just break down and have a good cry. I suppose it's better than always crying at any time as I have learned when working that you cannot let your personal problems get in the way.

Prior to Dad's passing, I had been spearheading the planning of my ten-year high school reunion, to be held in July. That kept me busy and helped me cope with his passing, but once August rolled around, I no longer had a convenient distraction. I only had work to think about, and it was a slow month. My energy levels dropped dramatically, I was lethargic, and I only wanted to sleep. This went on for a month, and I knew things were not normal. Instead of seeking treatment from someone, I stumbled on an article about depression causing you to be very tired, and I instantly knew I was depressed.

I don't know how my own diagnosis snapped me out of it, but the next day, I was pretty much back to normal. I realized I still hadn't mourned Dad's death, but I figured there was no real manual on how to do that. I got through it by living my life to the best of my ability and reminding myself that I wasn't going to get over it instantly.

It was hard to pick up the pieces without Dad. As with many fathers, he was the one to gather the family. We grew up camping on Oahu's North Shore. Although I always dreaded it because I did not like sleeping in a sleeping bag or in a tent, looking back, I realize it was a good place to relax, enjoy nature, and hang out with family and friends. Dad also had designated specific nights we had dinner as a family.

The first few years after his passing, my mom tried to keep up with all the traditions, but it got difficult as her mobility declined. The holidays were especially tough. I cried a lot that first New Year's Eve without my dad. Setting off fireworks and eating cultural foods was a popular New Year's Eve tradition in my family. Ever since I can remember, Dad would gather us for the New Year's Day party. I thought 2004 was a difficult year, but it was only the beginning of what was to come.

To every life there is a death. Although there is never anything that can prepare us for when that day comes, what we will feel when it happens, and how it will impact our lives, it's a cycle we must accept. As hard as it is to deal with loss, especially when it's someone close to us, we will ultimately be all right. Although we will never be fully complete without the person in our lives and we will always wish we could bring that person back, if we keep their memory close to our heart, let go, and find joy in our current life, we allow ourselves to be in a better place.

Adjusting to Change and Moving On

Many times, people feel lost and unable to move on after tragedy strikes, but would the person who is gone ever wish to leave their family behind or have their family unable to deal with the loss and move on with their lives? The closer the person is to you and the more you depended on them, the harder it can be. But even in darkness, there is light. Following each storm, there is eventually sunshine.

In January of 2005, I was promoted to district sales coordinator. After being with the supplemental-insurance company for little more than a year, I felt like that was a great accomplishment. I moved into the state office downtown and hired a part-time administrator. I took my business and my work very seriously, always doing my best to put myself in a position to grow and succeed. In 2005, I won countless awards for my second year in the business, as well as multiple awards as a manager. I was proud of myself and what I accomplished through hard work and perseverance.

On the home front, I was adjusting to life without my dad and helping my mom. My grandfather was having a difficult time being alone after losing my grandma in 2003, and where he never owned a home, we decided that instead of him paying rent to someone else, he should move in with us. The kindest man, Grandpa had always been a big part of my life, and I was so glad to be able to spend more time with him.

In spite of the recent loss of my grandmother and father, this was the least stressful period of my life. I didn't really have anyone to be accountable to, work was growing and wasn't really stressful, and I still had family that could help me. This was the year Jason and I decided to start our family.

After work, I would come home and take a good nap because pregnancy made me tired. I would get up in time to eat dinner, which Mom or Grandpa cooked. Jason worked a swing shift as a massage therapist at a hotel, so he ate at work and was never home for dinner. Those were the simple days. As my life has become more and more complicated, I sometimes wish I could go back to where Mom was still functional and that my grandfather was alive and cooking for me, always asking me how I was doing, and telling me how proud he was of me.

"Time heals all wounds." It's true if we allow ourselves to grieve, accept what has happened, and continue to move forward. There are things that happen in our lives that can seem impossible to accept or move on from, but when we cannot ultimately control or avoid something happening, the focus should be on What now? How do we continue to live our lives to the fullest, and how will our loss impact who we can be in the future?

Leah

Bringing a child into the world is a miracle we often take for granted, but the pain and sorrow one experiences at the loss of a family member brings into sharper focus the joy we feel when our family is blessed with new life. It's one of the best gifts we can receive. With the loss of my father, I was looking forward to having a new family member.

During my pregnancy, I was able to maintain the same routine. If there was one thing I learned from my dad at a young age, it was discipline. Every day, he'd wake up at 4:30 a.m. and head to the YMCA. I developed the same habit and got up at 5:30 a.m. without fail to go to the gym. There was never an excuse not to go. I worked out five days a week and was in good shape my entire pregnancy.

My daughter, Leah, was the first grandchild on both sides. She is a carefree, happy, personable, kind soul. Her grandparents were in their fifties when she was born and were still working. Jason and I took turns watching my daughter during the day, and Mom helped us a little at night for the first year and a half while she was capable. Together, we were able to watch my daughter without a sitter the first year and a half. My in-laws moved to Japan about a year after she was born and stayed there for three years due to my father-in-law's work. At eighteen months, we decided it would be beneficial to find Leah a babysitter so she could be around other kids.

While the babysitter was a good decision, our plans for her to stay there until starting school were instantly interrupted. At two and a half, Leah's babysitter moved to a new house that did not permit her to watch the same number of children. As a result, she went from watching six kids to two, and my daughter was released. So we adjusted our schedules and took care of her until she started preschool six months later. We were fortunate we got accepted by our preschool of choice last minute, and then by a good school district for elementary school. The timing and how everything worked out to where Leah was less than ten minutes away from the hospital and nursing home was a blessing. Since it was my responsibility to take and pick up Leah from school every day and also to care for Mom, it really helped that everything was nearby.

At five years of age, Leah played soccer for a couple of years, though she did not enjoy it because she does not like to run. Jason was an avid soccer player and was terribly disappointed to learn that she would not follow in his footsteps. A couple of years later, we enrolled her at the studio where I had taken dance. Leah takes classes in jazz, ballet, contemporary, and hip-hop. She enjoys dancing and has a passion for it.

When Leah was a toddler, she watched us take care of my mother's father as we brought food to his condo and later visited him at the nursing home. She's also watched me care for my mom for as long as she can remember. When my son was born with special needs, we had another person to care for. Her never-ending responsibilities as an older sister have given her a perspective different from many of her peers. She is caring and compassionate and will lead a special and fulfilling life.

Leah brought hope and joy into our lives. It seemed we were blessed with a bright, beautiful rainbow to compensate for our recent stormy skies. But the weather was to change once again, and my small reprieve started to fade within a few years as another storm loomed on the horizon.

Mom's Decline

Is it unrealistic to hope that your parents will take care of you no matter how old you are? Maybe because in some way, we always want to be a kid and be taken care of?

To know that we have an extra set of people who love us unconditionally and will always be there to help us. While I am grateful to still have my mom, the role reversal of me taking care of her occurred far too early in my life, at the age of 31.

Mom didn't exercise while I was growing up, but when I moved home from college, she got a gym membership with me at a large fitness club. She worked out long and hard and, amazingly, she ran the Honolulu Marathon in 2005 with almost no training. I'm not sure if the extra strain from running the marathon triggered the nerve loss, but it seemed to slowly start after that. One small sign was falling down a couple of times while traveling internationally. She tripped just walking, and one of her injuries sent her to the emergency room. Not realizing it at the time, we later learned that the loss of strength in her arms affected her coordination walking.

In 2007, Mom started to notice it was becoming difficult to raise her left arm. As her range of motion started to diminish, she became worried and went looking for answers. I don't know how many doctors she saw, but they eventually discovered that one of the bones in her back was pressing on her spine, and they felt that could be contributing to her loss of motion. The surgery to remove the bone ended up being a big mistake. Afterward, the nerve loss and ability to move did not improve, even with all the recommended postsurgical treatments and therapy. Thankfully, she never experienced pain. In fact, there were many things over the years that might have caused her to need pain medicine, but for whatever reason, she never felt pain.

The doctors in Hawaii couldn't figure out what was going on, and so she was referred to the Mayo Clinic in Rochester,

Minnesota, for a diagnosis and treatment. Fortunately, Mom's sister lived in Eagan, Minnesota, roughly an hour's drive from Rochester. Mom lived at my auntie's house, and my aunty graciously took care of her and drove her back and forth to the clinic.

Mom was diagnosed with multifocal motor neuropathy, a rare motor-neuron disease. She took numerous trips to the Mayo Clinic for expensive IVIG treatments, but after rounds and rounds of treatment with no results, she gave up and came home.

When she was away, I handled all her finances. I'd taken care of all her mail prior to her leaving, but at this point I was going through the junk mail too and even mail still coming to my dad years after his death. One day I noticed a thin envelope addressed to my dad from a life-insurance company. I opened it to find a privacy notice with a policy number at the top right corner of the letter. I thought it was strange because there was no reason a privacy letter should be sent to Dad—unless he had a policy. I told Mom I would call to find out what was happening.

It turned out Dad had a policy. I helped file the claim, and Mom ended up with a little over $16,000. Imagine finding $16,000 in your couch, under a mattress, or in a piece of mail. Apparently, Dad had a life-insurance policy he had canceled back in 1982, and it provided paid-up insurance which allowed Dad to have a small death benefit for a limited time without having to pay any premiums in the future. Since he hadn't paid for the policy since 1982, my dad didn't think he still had life insurance. The policy was going to expire in 2011. The death benefit was $12,000 plus interest since we hadn't collected the money when he passed away in 2004.

While $16,000 seems like a lot of money, from a life-insurance standpoint, it really isn't. My dad did not have an active policy that could help Mom, and we learned the hard way how much that impacts the surviving spouse and family. But I was thankful I had been inspired to look into this letter. I felt a deep spiritual connection after this because I knew I had been guided to this discovery.

Mom never went back to work after the surgery and treatments. The nerve loss accelerated so quickly she couldn't walk or even sit at a desk and type on the computer. Fortunately, she was able to collect temporary disability insurance (TDI) mandated by the state, requiring employers to pay when employees missed work for off-the-job injuries and illnesses. Although it paid only 58 percent of her income, it was something. She'd also accumulated six months of sick and vacation pay, which she cashed out. Before a year had passed, she had qualified for Social Security Disability payments which are extremely hard to qualify for because you have to prove you cannot go back to work in any occupation, ever. I currently work in employee benefits and know that many companies do not offer a lot of sick leave or vacation pay. In those cases, employees are left without pay and must struggle to pay their bills. I told her she was very fortunate.

When Mom first started losing range of motion, she had a hard time extending her left arm above her head. As time went on, she lost the use of not only her arms, but her legs. One thing I vividly remember as she lost her independence was how difficult everyday actions became. Even eating became a chore. She couldn't hold a metal utensil because it was too heavy, and we had to switch everything to plastic. At some point, she couldn't lift her fork from the plate to her mouth. She had to bend her head to the plate in order to put food into her mouth.

Gradually losing her freedom was heartbreaking for her and for those who loved her. Soon the day came when she knew she could no longer drive because she was unable to steer. Within about six months of stopping her treatments at the Mayo Clinic, she could no longer walk. Normally, someone who is unable to walk still has the use of their hands and arms. But without the ability to move her body, Mom was completely incapacitated and basically bedridden.

She was in her midfifties as this was happening. With the loss of movement, she became unable to do many of the things that defined her. She had been a good cook; everything she made was delicious. In her early twenties, she had a cookie company, and her chocolate chip cookies were renowned. They were crunchy yet filled with sweet and gooey chocolate chips. She was always making cookies and giving them away, especially during the holidays. She also made the best butter mochi. In the center of each mochi was a bit of melt-in-your-mouth heaven. The outside edges had an almost-burnt crunchiness everyone craved. She was a true artist when it came to the kitchen, and I am deeply saddened she will never cook again.

When I was younger, my creative, multitalented mother would enter gift-wrapping contests during Christmas at the hotel she worked for and often won first or second place. When jewelry-making became a fad, Mom stockpiled beads and supplies. She was self-taught, because YouTube didn't exist back then.

She also loved to knit and crochet her own sweaters. I never took the time the learn what she was doing, but I was always fascinated by how she did it all by hand. For my wedding, Mom knit different colored lei for all the women in the family. It was wonderful to see my mother-in-law, the grandmas, and the aunties wearing them. It saddens me to think she can't use her talents anymore. In fact, sometimes I think I'm sadder than she is because she never complains or talks about what she used to do and cannot do any longer.

Mom was pretty and always wore makeup, jewelry, and nice clothes. I don't think I ever saw her in a T-shirt and shorts, unless it was to work out or go camping. As Mom lost her ability to move, she could not do her makeup and stopped wearing it. Her ability to keep up her appearance has diminished, but her skin still glows, her hair is beautiful, and her countenance radiates with an inner beauty.

It's scary to think that our health can change overnight and without warning. Even the healthiest of people can experience cancer, heart attacks, or neuromuscular diseases. Mom went from never getting sick or missing work to being completely disabled. I had never thought it possible, and that's what's scary for me—given the stress levels and the physical demands that come with caring for a son with special needs, what might happen if my health were to suddenly decline?

While I know I'm not invincible and that anything can happen, I have learned a few things from my family experiences. One, take good care of yourself. Two, make sure you have some form of income and insurance in place. Three, pace yourself and live each day as if it matters because you don't know when it will be your last.

CHAPTER 3

Are We Ever Really Prepared for What Tomorrow Brings?

The Long-Term-Care Journey

If I ever end up in a care home, just shoot me because I would rather be dead." Sound far-fetched? Believe it or not, I have heard it several times over the years in my discussions with others about long-term care. Nobody wants to lose the ability to take care of themselves. It's one of the hardest things for not only the person losing their independence but also the people who help care for them. But just because we cannot fully care for ourselves does not mean our life does not still have value, that we are no longer loved, or that we should be removed from this earth.

As Mom's mobility declined, we had to figure out how to take care of her. Since I lived with her, I drove her places while she could still walk. Once she lost that ability, I helped with cooking, cleaning, shopping, calling people, etc. I also continued to handle her finances.

By 2008, I advised Mom we should start using her long-term-care policy because she needed assistance with more than two of the six daily-living activities needed to activate the policy. She resisted me for at least six months because she didn't know how her policy worked, despite me telling her.

I learned about long-term-care insurance when I first started selling insurance in 2003. I'd watched my grandfather take care of my grandmother for three years until her passing in 2003. I saw how much work it was, and I wanted to make sure Mom could be cared for if she ever needed it. Since my dad was sick at the time, I couldn't get him coverage, but I sold Mom a policy right away. Little did I know that six years later, Mom would file a claim. Although long-term-care insurance is slowly disappearing and the industry has drastically changed over the last ten years or so, it can be one of the best investments. A policy that will pay potentially hundreds of thousands or even millions of dollars of benefits means financial peace of mind in providing the best care for a loved one. It was one of the best financial decisions we ever made.

We paid only $89 a month for Mom's policy for six years before she filed a claim for a total of $6,408. The starting monthly benefit payout was $200 a day or $6,000 a month. It had a 5 percent compound-inflation rider on it, which meant the benefit went up by 5 percent a year on the increased benefit amount, not the starting benefit amount. After one year, $6,000 a month turned into $6,300 a month, then $6,615 a month, then $6,945.75 a month, then $7,293.04 a month, $7,657.69 a month, and $8,040.57 a month. Or on a daily benefit, $200 a day turned into $210, $220.50, $231.53, $243.10, $255.26, $268.02, and $281.42. By the time Mom activated her claim, it was already paying at a rate of $281.42 a day.

To provide her with some general care, we brought in a caregiver two to four hours a day to help with things like bathing, dressing, brushing teeth, feeding, changing diapers or the bedpan, light cleaning, etc. The agencies we used at the time were charging $22 to $24 an hour plus tax for this type of care. We were being billed about $50 to $100 a day. Mom's policy had an indemnity versus a reimbursement payout, which meant that as long as she used care that day, she collected the whole daily payout, not just what she was charged. If she incurred a charge of only $50, she still got the $281.42 a day.

We didn't use care every day at first, but eventually Mom realized she was making money and getting the care she needed at the same time. It was a huge relief for her to have extra money besides her Social Security and pension income, and it was a huge relief for us because we didn't have to feel guilty about spending money on her care.

We used the in-home-care part of her long-term-care policy for around two and a half years before her care level increased. I had a hard time dealing with Mom's decline in mobility and loss of independence. As a caregiver, I wasn't frustrated with helping her, I was frustrated because I felt bad that she couldn't do anything on her own and had to constantly rely on others. Working with a severely disabled loved one gave me a much deeper appreciation of my own life and abilities.

Many people need care for a severe cognitive impairment, such as Alzheimer's and dementia. Caring for someone with severe short-term memory loss often means constant vigilance and extreme mental fatigue and worry. What if their loved one leaves the house and gets lost or forgets to turn the stove off? And it's mentally exhausting to have to repeat something five times because the person you're caring for doesn't remember they asked the same question just two minutes prior. And what of the heartache that comes when the cognitively impaired family member no longer recognizes them?

As we learn to embrace the physical and mental changes a loved one is experiencing, it is important for us to find balance, mentally and emotionally. There will be moments of sadness. If our parents were our heroes growing up, we want to remember them at their best, not in their moments of weakness.

As unpleasant as it may be for a caretaker to witness the decline of their loved one, we must remember who the person we're caring for is before we reject them or think of them as an inconvenience. Often, they don't want to be a burden to anyone, let alone their loved ones. But, ultimately, they have limited control of the situation. As a caregiver, keep an open mind, talk to others if you're having difficulty emotionally processing the changes, and always see your loved one for who they are, not for what they can or cannot do.

Changing Careers

A job is something you do to earn money; a career is something you do for a significant period of time that you hope will lead to opportunities and success. When you build a career, you're building a foundation to grow upon; you're not looking to be a peg on the board that can be moved or removed at any time. When you change jobs, you are changing the place you work. When you change careers, you are branching out to build another opportunity for yourself.

Taking care of Mom was an additional task on my plate, but I didn't let it prevent me from making changes in my life. Confident that I would be able to handle anything thrown my way, I continued to search for ways to build my career.

I was grateful to have built a large book of business and to have gained a lot of experience as a district sales coordinator for the supplemental-insurance company. Since 2005, I had been a large producer and managed a team of commission-only salespeople. I started the position super excited to teach people sales skills and to build a successful team of agents, and I thought managing people would be easy because everyone could succeed with training and tools. But I learned a lot about people, their personalities, and their work ethic. Early on, I had a few agents who learned my methods, worked hard, and were growing their business.

Over time, however, it became a revolving door, and as my personal life got more complicated, I did not want to have to take care of more people than I already was. Since I worked with independent agents, I could not control what someone did in a day or fire them for not doing their work. The lack of control and the lack of effort on other people's parts became mentally exhausting.

Changes were coming on the management levels. The expectations related to a manager's focus and responsibility started to shift away from how I had structured my business. I am more proactive than reactive, and although I didn't have to make changes, I thought it would be better to initiate change instead of being forced to change at some point.

When you're self-employed, part of building your career is determining which direction to go and what to focus on. Stepping down from being a manager was not a logical thing to do unless I had another strategy, as that would have been going backward instead of forward. I began to contemplate, analyze, research, discuss, throw it out to the universe, brainstorm, and figure out what kind of change would take me upward.

I circled back to my dream of becoming a financial advisor. Was I confident enough that I could succeed? Did I have enough courage to take a leap of faith? If I lost income from overrides as a manager with my current job, would I be able to recoup that income as an advisor, and how long would it take me to start making money? The prospect of working for myself in a straight-commission world with expenses such as an office and administrator required deep consideration. It wasn't like I could just leave one employer and start with another without some fallout, but I decided to move ahead.

Once I made up my mind, I was given an opportunity to work with a successful advisor who co-owned a small local advisory firm. Being an advisor meant I would need to get my securities licenses in addition to the life and health insurance licenses I already had. The challenge was that I worked forty-plus-hour weeks, had a young daughter, took care of Mom a couple of days a week, and wanted to have a second child. I would need to find time to study for two very difficult exams. There were a few different test options, but I was told to go for the top licenses and get it all over with. I really had no idea what I was getting myself into or how hard the tests would be, but I moved forward anyway.

To prepare for my Series 7 and Series 66 exams, I used a company that offered an in-person crash course in Los Angeles, California, as well as online practice tests. The

Series 7 book was three hundred pages long, with twenty-one chapters of condensed material in an outline format. With no investment experience other than my 401(k), I was not familiar with calls, options, puts, or any of the jargon associated with the profession. Thinking that taking the class for a week in person would help me with the study material, I booked a ticket to LA and paid for the one-week course.

I arrived at my hotel in LA feeling lost, alone, crazy, insecure, stupid, and scared. I didn't open the book until I arrived at the five-day class, and I walked out feeling more confused than when I walked in. Most of the people in the class had either studied the material before, were taking the test a second time, worked at a firm where they were around this information, or had already passed the Series 6 exam and weren't completely lost on the Series 7 material. I could have taken the Series 6 exam, which was simpler and would have allowed me to invest in mutual funds, but I would not be able to work with managed accounts, stocks, ETF's, etc., without my Series 7 license.

I came back from the class in early 2010 and evaluated my schedule and the material I would need to learn to pass this test. There were practice tests for each chapter and cumulative tests at the end. I needed a 70 percent to pass. Jason, Leah, and had I scheduled a trip to Japan in early April to visit my in-laws. I wanted to make sure I passed the test before our trip and get my taxes done by April 15. Another reason I wanted to pass right away was because I wanted to get pregnant. Should I take all my tests before getting pregnant, while I was pregnant, or after giving birth? I hoped to pass my exams before I got pregnant.

I managed to find the hundreds of hours needed to study for the exam by waking up and studying the book outlines and practice tests while working out on the elliptical at home, and I studied a couple of hours at work and one to two hours before bedtime. On weekends, I took the practice tests in my home office. Because the test contained so much material and I didn't have the luxury of studying all day, there was no way I could take it after just three weeks. It wasn't easy to remember the material I'd studied in earlier chapters six to eight weeks later while I was studying later chapters. I was terrified my brain would not be capable of retaining all the information required to pass.

As my test date approached, my practice scores were between sixty-six and seventy-four percent, and I needed a seventy to pass. I was not trying to get a ninety; I just wanted to pass. Multiple-choice tests were never my forte. If anything, they scared me. I didn't feel completely ready, but I didn't know if I could move my exam back any further on such short notice as I needed to pass it before my trip, so I chanced it, took the test—and missed passing by one question. I needed to get 175 questions right, and I got 174. My results said the national average was a low—73 percent—and only 66 percent of the people passed. I couldn't believe it. It was the hardest I'd ever studied for a test, and I had missed passing by one question! I was devastated. What was frustrating about failing was that I was not allowed to reschedule my test for thirty days. That was thirty days before I could jump on the website to *schedule* it, not take it.

When I returned from Japan, I went back to studying and rescheduled the exam. I was on top of the world when I got a high score. It was a major accomplishment to pass such a difficult exam with everything I had on my plate, and I was proud of myself for not giving up. While I believe intelligence has different forms and I feel blessed to have a variety of skills and abilities, I wouldn't call myself intelligent when it comes to test-taking. While studying for the Series 7 exam, I taught myself test-taking techniques and gained more confidence in passing the multiple-choice tests. Where my career requires me to continually take tests for compliance, continuing education, and designations, I'm glad my test-taking skills have improved.

The Series 7 exam was the longer and harder exam. Having finished that, I thought I could get pregnant and study for the Series 66 with the goal of passing it before the end of 2010. Since we loved our first trip to Japan, we decided to return in early October for another visit to my in-laws. The Tuesday before we left, I went in for my thirteen-week checkup. My doctor discovered there was no heartbeat—and no baby. I was shocked. What happened? How could the baby have just disappeared?

The OBGYN said that since the baby had not washed out, I would need to have a D&C or I risked excessive bleeding. I was leaving on Thursday for ten days, and I did not want that to happen in a foreign country, so we scheduled an emergency D&C. I went to the hospital, received anesthesia, had the surgery, and went home to finish packing. I got on a plane the following day.

It was nice to be in Japan, where I could escape the world and be taken care of by my in-laws—something I hadn't had from my own parents in a long time—but it was a very emotional trip. My hormones were raging and I was crying most of the time, but I knew I couldn't let the loss consume me. I knew miscarriages were common, especially within the first thirteen weeks, but I didn't think it would happen to me. I don't think anyone does. If I still wanted a second child, I needed to heal and move forward.

When I came back, I had to take my Series 66 test. I had been studying for it and felt confident I could pass with over a 70. I took it in late October and thought I'd passed until I saw my score. It said I had gotten a 73—and failed. I freaked out, baffled at why I had not passed. It turned out I needed a 75. The testing company I had used to study had not disclosed that information. In fact, the practice exams gave you a green if you were good, a yellow if you were borderline, or a red if you were failing, the color system based on a 70 being the passing score.

When I called them on it, they refused to admit their error or refund my money. I was furious. I learned from the Series 7 exam that if I wasn't ready, postponing the exam another week was smarter than not passing and waiting thirty days to reschedule. If I was given accurate information, I would not have made the same mistake again. I already had such a trying year having just miscarried and taken the Series 7 exam twice. I was frustrated, irritated, stressed, and anxious about not passing the test.

But it wasn't in me to give up on something when I was seriously committed to it. It was late October, and I could not schedule my exam for thirty days, and yet my peak enrollment season at work was November–December. I was so busy I couldn't fathom having to pass another test. But I had a goal in mind, so I had no choice. In early December, I took the test knowing what was on the line. The questions were so difficult I had major anxiety. It seemed as if every question had two right answers. I thought I was going to lose my mind. Waiting for the results to pop up at the end seemed like the longest minute of my life. I thought I would have a heart attack. But as God and fate would have it, I passed!

Being properly licensed in 2010 meant I could continue broadening and changing the scope of what I was doing. I left my downtown office, and in 2011, moved into the building of the advising firm I was partnering with. They didn't have room in their office for both my administrator and me, so I leased my own office. Right away, I felt like a fish out of water. They didn't provide much in the way of training—I was only trained on things on an as-needed basis or if I asked because they didn't have training systems set up, and training outside of cases took up valuable time.

I quickly realized that advising was nothing like selling supplemental insurance. I had to ask my current clients if they had an advisor, and if not, did they want to work with me? However, I was not confident enough in this new endeavor or in the process. I wrote script after script, hoping to feel more comfortable approaching prospective clients. Ultimately, I couldn't wing advising like I could supplemental insurance, and even though I had a lot of insurance clients, I didn't have the confidence to convert them right away.

I decided to seek out other firms that offered more training. Long story short, I moved to a company that provided good training and allowed me to keep and run my employee-benefits business while pursuing my quest to be a financial advisor. In August, I began to learn the advising company's products and systems and listened to their training sessions. Since the products, applications, and systems were all new, it took time to build my sales.

Growing my financial-advising business was more difficult than I imagined. It was nothing like selling supplemental insurance. *Everything* was different and much harder, but I made the switch and didn't look back, regardless of what happened to be on my plate, and I eventually got my insurance clients to become my financial-planning clients.

Sometimes I'm amazed at how I test myself and take leaps of faith. In retrospect, I think when you allow yourself to reach for more meaningful, impactful goals, it helps settle the fears and doubts that creep into your mind, telling you that you cannot do it. As Rome was not built in a day, neither is any long-term foundation. The most solid foundations take time to build and are often tested along the way. The true test of perseverance is reaching your end goal no matter what happens.

When giving up is not an option and failure is not permanent, you have no choice but to succeed, no matter how long it takes. You *can* change your circumstances, no matter how bad your life has been. I tell people who have experienced rough times that things can only get better and that they can change their trajectory in life if they'll make the effort. Yesterday is gone, and we don't know when our tomorrow will end, so why not make the most of today?

Two Tragedies in One Month

Have you ever seen where one tragedy happens after another, whether directly related to each other or not? How can we truly be prepared when we don't see something coming?

My maternal grandfather was distant from us growing up as he was quiet and kept to himself. Grandpa went to my dad for massage and vitamin supplements. He was a healthy and strong old man up until 2008, when he fell at his apartment and couldn't get up. For a couple of years, Mom stocked his refrigerator weekly. One day she'd come to replenish his supplies and found him on the floor, stuck between the couch and the coffee table. Unable to get up, he was almost nonresponsive from not eating or drinking for nearly a week. As a result, his kidneys were failing and he had to go to dialysis for months until his kidneys recovered.

He was lucky to be alive. With Grandpa's health in jeopardy, Mom knew he could no longer stay at home alone, and so the decision was made to put him in a nursing home. For the next few years, on Saturdays, Mom and I would take my grandpa's sister to run errands and then visit my grandpa. Mom was no longer able to drive, so I was her chauffeur. I didn't mind helping because doing the right thing or what was expected of me to help family was more rewarding than any recreational activity. I've always had a deep sense of familial obligation and commitment. Since I was helping Mom help my grandfather, I saw him more in the last three years of his life than I had the whole thirty years of my life prior to that point.

In September 2011, Grandpa passed away at the age of ninety-two. At his funeral service, Mom was very sickly and weak. She was skin and bones and had dwindled to sixty-four pounds. Because she couldn't breathe, she barely made it through the service. Afterward, we took her to the hospital and found out she had aspiration pneumonia. They gave her an IV to treat the pneumonia, and from there it was a waiting game. She was so malnourished the doctors were concerned about her nutrition and temporarily installed a G-tube (gastrointestinal) in her stomach. Because we knew that people died from pneumonia all the time, we knew it was serious. But I was hopeful that, with time, she would get better and come back home.

Mom had been in the hospital for two days when I received a call midmorning saying she had a "code blue" and was being rushed to ICU. I had no clue what a code blue was but had a sinking feeling it meant she had died. The hospital staff explained that she'd gone into cardiopulmonary arrest, but they'd been able to get her breathing again. She was stabilized for the moment, but I needed to come to the ICU as soon as possible. I dropped whatever I had planned for the rest of the day and rushed to the hospital.

Although I knew Mom was very ill, I was still shocked by the turn of events. As I rushed to the hospital, I recalled her telling me the day prior that she couldn't breathe when the nurses had laid her flat to change her. Although she'd let them know, I suppose the information had not been relayed to the other nurses, who must have unknowingly laid her flat. I was upset. This mistake had almost cost Mom her life and certainly changed her future and what care would be required moving forward.

When I arrived at the ICU, I was told to wait outside her room. My mind was in a whirl, my heart was racing, and I was breathing hard. I wasn't ready to lose her. I felt so alone and scared. When I eventually did get to see her, I remember breathing a momentary sigh of relief that she was alive. She had tubes everywhere and looked extremely out of it, but she was fine—for now. She wasn't crying, stressed out, or emotional. I, on the other hand, was freaking out, fearing she wouldn't make it out of the hospital alive.

I was told we had to make a decision because they could only leave the tube in for a couple of days. The choice was between hospice and a tracheotomy. This was the first of many stressful decisions. I experienced so many extreme emotions the first day she was in the ICU, thinking she might die. When I tried to communicate with her to find out what she wanted, she could not respond. There was not a single thing in her body that moved or worked. She couldn't lift a finger, let alone write; she couldn't talk with the tube in her mouth; she even couldn't gesture with her arms or nod. I was forced to try and read her eyes. I asked for alphabet boards or boards that showed images depicting changing the TV channel, being hungry, using the bathroom, etc., which were helpful, but the picture boards were of no use when the conversation was about putting in a tracheotomy or going to hospice.

As much as I felt she might be near the end, I knew she didn't think she was dying, nor did she want to die. While her original health-care directive said to not prolong life, I knew she wanted any treatment that could help keep her alive. She did not want to be left to die in hospice, and she didn't think she needed the tracheotomy because she thought she could still breathe on her own. She felt her situation was mainly due to the pneumonia. We found ourselves having to make a life-or-death decision.

Reaching this understanding between us took a great deal of time and effort. I stood by her bed trying to figure out what she was thinking. I would point to the letters on the board, compose sentences, and ask if that was correct, doing just about anything to have a conversation with her. Getting a complete thought out of her took at least half an hour. It was the most nerve-wracking thing I had ever experienced until that point in time, and I was now five months pregnant. Standing for hours at a time trying to interpret Mom's thoughts required an incredible amount of focus and stamina. It was exhausting to have to do it every evening after a long day of work.

It took a long time for her pneumonia to clear up, and once it did, we needed to wait even longer because the nursing home wouldn't take patients with a trach less than thirty days old. I didn't really think about the extra stress and strain it was putting on me, my body, and my baby. I just knew I needed to be there for Mom. I knew we were in for some changes as Mom would require twenty-four-hour care from that point moving forward.

In addition, Mom was trustee for my grandfather's trust. Since he'd just passed away and she didn't expect to be fighting for her life, she decided it was safer to transfer that duty to me. I was already her trustee, and she wanted to make sure someone took care of his trust. I was tasked with finding a notary who knew what to do when a person was unable to sign something themselves and who could meet us at the hospital. I then had to work on settling his trust, and all the extra stress was wearing on me.

I felt bad for Mom. If she hadn't contracted pneumonia, things would have been different, and there's a chance she wouldn't have needed a trach. I learned to suction her over the years, and though it seems like it would be uncomfortable to have a plastic tube shoved down your throat and then pulled back up to get the saliva and mucus out, the trach kept her from getting pneumonia again.

After her close call with death, Mom was paranoid that the nurses would leave her to die again. The code blue had been caused by the hospital's negligence. Mom had previously never worried that she might die, but after this experience, she developed a deep fear. She realized that an airway obstruction could be fatal, and she really didn't want to go. She wanted to see her second grandchild.

In the intensive care unit, there was one nurse for every two patients. They were very attentive and always in and out of her room, but hospitals only allow patients to remain in an intensive care unit for so long. When she was transferred to a regular room after a few days, she told me she wanted me to hire someone to watch her twenty-four hours a day. Their instructions were to stay alert, to closely watch her face, and, if she made any kind of facial gesture indicating that she needed something, they were to find out what she needed, like calling a nurse or respiratory therapist to provide suction. I asked the hospital if they were all right with that. I think they thought I was a little crazy, but they approved. I was grateful because it relieved Mom's fear of suffocating.

Finding people and making sure they showed up was not easy. The agencies sent people who could stay with Mom overnight. I couldn't do it. No matter how much I loved Mom, I had my own family. Plus, I needed my sleep. Even at the best of times, if I didn't get at least five hours of decent sleep in a bed, I was not functional the next day. And between my pregnancy and the extreme stress I was under, I needed to sleep in my own bed so I didn't jeopardize my health or that of the baby.

Following Mom's near-death experience at the hospital, we activated the nursing-home portion of her long-term-care policy. During her first six months at the nursing home, we had twenty-four-hour in-home care. It seemed crazy to be so vigilant, but just like when she was in the hospital, she needed someone in the room with her to relieve her anxiety of suffocating. I would head to the nursing home daily and communicate with the caregiving agencies to make sure their people were showing up to take care of her.

Being in charge of her care and finances was like having another job on top of my jobs as a business owner, mother, and wife. There was a lot of pressure in coordinating her care over the years. It's not as involved as physically doing the care yourself, but caring for someone with disabilities requires specific accommodations and considerations. And any such responsibility can impact a person physically, mentally, emotionally, and financially. Caregivers must have a way to get rest, find balance, and release stress. If you find yourself on autopilot, take breaks every so often where you can get away and regroup to find your sanity and to refresh your mind and spirit. My guess is that many of you reading this book have gone through similar situations. I give you a lot of credit, a pat on the back, and hope that you may have the strength you need to continue to do all you do. For those who have not yet experienced caring for a disabled loved one, I hope you will be strong and capable if and when the time arrives.

Coordinating Care

A research company did a comprehensive article on long-term-care statistics. I am not quoting anything as those numbers are always changing, but the reality is that we are living longer because of medical advances, and the increasing number of people who will need long-term care is startling. It's common to be told that if you're sixty-five or older, you have a more than a 50 percent chance of needing care. In fact, if you're reading this book, you or someone in your family has probably cared for someone or you know someone else who has.

At the time, caring for Mom in 2008, I was still thirty-one years old. I had a young child at home and was trying to build my career. I would like to say it was somewhat gradual, but Mom's deterioration came on quickly. Her care started with handling all of her finances because it got difficult for her to write and sign her name. With that came the coordination of long-term-care services and insurance payments. I always made her mortgage payments and transferred money at the banks. To this day, I still handle all of her finances, although it's nothing like it used to be.

I started coordinating in-home care for Mom in 2009, working with three caregiving agencies because one could not always accommodate us. It was a rather frustrating process. People would frequently show up late while the person on the current shift needed to leave, and Mom would become deeply fearful if left alone for even thirty minutes. There were also times when, for one reason or another, she didn't like the caregiver. I would have to tell the agency quite frequently not to send a particular caregiver back. When she did find someone she liked, it was rare that this person was always available because of scheduling issues. The frustrating part about inconsistent caregivers was she always had to reexplain what she wanted and hope that person would do it to her liking.

For many reasons, I chose to have her long-term-care insurance pay us directly instead of paying the caregiving agencies. However, that meant I had to review the bills monthly with Mom to make sure they were accurate before submitting them to the long-term-care insurance company for payment. In addition to paying her bills and handling all of her finances, I had to keep track of all her care-coordination scheduling, billings, payments, and reimbursements. Needless to say, I was always on the phone with the caregiving agencies about scheduling her care. The stressful part about coordinating her care was making sure she was never stranded and was always taken care of.

My brother and I sacrificed a lot to make sure she received the best care. I lived with Mom up until August of 2009. Once I moved out and Jason and I bought our house, my brother and his partner moved in with her. While I handled her finances, my brother and his partner helped Mom during the hours we didn't have caregivers coming to the house, and they took her on errands. They helped with her physical care too. We all experienced changing her and giving her baths. Since Mom lost all her nerves and muscles, it was like lifting dead weight, but we did what we had to. When you selflessly care for someone, you must put aside any awkward and uncomfortable feelings. You focus on compassion and provide help to express gratitude for the sacrifices that person made for you over the years. My brother and his partner were good about helping with Mom's physical needs, and it was a blessing having them at the house.

Mom is still bedridden today. It's hard to describe having a parent who's not capable of doing anything. She couldn't even move a strand of hair off her face or scratch her nose. Once Mom was in the nursing home and I stopped coordinating caregivers from the agency to watch her, my job got a little easier. However, my financial and personal responsibilities didn't end there.

When it comes to caring for a parent or loved one, no matter the person's limitations, there's always some type of physical burden placed on those who care for them. This physical burden often affects the caregiver's health and can wear the body down. And it's tough to see your parent in a diminished capacity, whether physically or cognitively. It's heartbreaking when they can no longer do what they used to and when they cannot remember you or they ask you to repeat something five times.

It can be financially stressful to have to pay a caregiver or nursing home or sacrifice work hours and income in order to have the time and energy needed to care for a loved one. There's a whirlwind of guilt that constantly surrounds you because of the choices and sacrifices you must make. Once a loved one must depend on you, you face some tough choices.

Many of my clients are facing the task of caring for a loved one. Most of the time, it's their parents. We talk about what they're going through, and I often give them advice on things to consider and perspective on their situations. What's sad is when the client has siblings who could help care for the parent, but the burden falls solely on them. The siblings feel like they are incapable of enduring the physical, mental, and emotional challenges of caring for a parent. I'm not sure how those who refuse to help can justify it, other than feeling like they're too busy or have their own set of problems. Personally, I've always been "too busy" and had my own set of problems, but I could never use that as an excuse.

I simply learned to prioritize who and what I had to take care of based on urgency. I was constantly going back and forth and worrying about what would require my attention each day. The more you have on your plate and the more things you must take care of, the harder it is to juggle everything. I felt like I was constantly juggling a dozen balls. Sometimes I had to focus on one ball more than others, especially when things were life-threatening or had deadlines.

Many days, I couldn't predict what would happen, and what I'd planned would change because someone needed me. It was a good thing I was my own boss because I didn't have to answer to anyone or ask permission to take care of anyone who needed me. I worked whenever I could; in fact, I found a way to work forty-plus hours a week. I didn't stay at the office until late, but I would frequently work from my home office. It became second nature to do whatever I could do when I could do it.

I believe you can do anything for a short time—for instance, skimping on sleep—and avoid negative side effects, but no one can keep that up without paying a price. My mantra has always been to be there but to pace yourself. In my situation, it is not a sprint, it's a marathon. Your health and well-being should be a priority.

While there are many conflicting opinions about caring for loved ones, I feel that everyone is entitled to their own opinions and choices. But I have to admit, things are much harder than they appear, and planning for what could happen can help you be ready when situations arise.

Mom's life completely changed after she was released from the hospital. Now that she had a tracheotomy and was on a ventilator, going home was not an option. She had to be placed in a nursing home. When you think of a nursing home providing twenty-four-hour care, it does, to an extent, but nobody is with your loved one twenty-four hours a day.

Given Mom's fear of being alone and suffocating, we ended up using three call mechanisms. One was a flat push button positioned perfectly behind her head so she could press it. Another was a doorbell button taped to a slab of wood set near one of her toes. And then she bought a Tobii computer for $10,000, which had an alarm button. Tobii computers are designed to help those with disabilities and include eye-tracking to assist with limited mobility. Mom's range of motion in her hands was limited to one centimeter.

If the cursor from the mouse was not directly over the alarm button, she couldn't move it. Thus, having multiple call mechanisms was important. If the first one didn't get a response and she really needed someone, she would go to the second and the third and keep ringing the bells. As she grew more confident that help would arrive, I stopped hiring caregivers to come to the nursing home.

While a nursing home is expensive, paying a caregiver by the hour for a twenty-four-hour period is much more. Thankfully, long-term-care insurance covered the cost of Mom's room in the nursing home, and she was fortunate to have good medical insurance. The financial peace of mind she had during the whole process was priceless and made taking care of her a little easier. It was reassuring to know that trained people were caring for her.

Everyone's situation is different in terms of financial and physical resources, able bodies, and schedules. Sometimes we don't have any family that can help, and sometimes family may live in another state, where it's logistically impossible to help without disrupting someone's life. Sometimes people must work and have their own families to take care of, which limits their ability to take care of a loved one.

Sometimes the level of care requires more skill than a family has. Sometimes the care is too physical and can wear down a caregiver. Sometimes it's too mentally or emotionally draining. And while caregiving may be a difficult subject to contemplate, it's important to plan ahead of time with those who may be involved. My hope for anyone who needs care in the future is that their loved ones take seriously the responsibility of seeing that they are adequately cared for.

CHAPTER 4

Only When It's Dark Can You See the Stars

Jett

If you're fortunate enough to be blessed with a child, the question you are often asked is when you are going to have a second. Some people time their children a certain number of years apart. Others randomly pop one child out after another. And there are those with children so far apart in age it may seem totally unplanned. I knew I wanted two children, but there were a lot of moving parts between work, taking care of Mom, and my living situation—all of which snowballed after my daughter was born.

After my miscarriage in 2010, my body needed to go through several cycles to fully recover. Blood tests revealed that an egg had attached a couple of times but the baby was lost early on. My body was messed up after the miscarriage and D&C, but there was nothing I could do at that point. Then, about six to seven months after my miscarriage, I got pregnant again. Based on the measurement of the baby, at my four-week appointment, I was told my due date was February 6. But by my calculations, where you got the due date from your last period, I felt their estimation was two weeks late.

My first trimester went well. The baby was growing, and its heart rate was strong. However, after thirteen weeks, I became uncomfortable. I was carrying the baby low, and there was a pressure on my stomach that made it difficult to exercise, so I stopped exercising even though that was difficult for me. Women make a lot of sacrifices during pregnancy.

Exercise was important to me because it helped release endorphins and mitigate stress. I exercised for that reason as well as to maintain my health, weight, and feel somewhat good about my body. I wasn't blessed with a fast metabolism or what some might call "good genes." I've always struggled with my weight as I am curvy, and I felt chubby off and on throughout my life. It's hard to recollect exactly how I felt during pregnancy because I was pretty distracted with changing financial-planning firms and Mom's month-long hospitalization.

The stress I felt during my second pregnancy was not ideal; however, I did my best to take care of myself. Everything seemed to be on track, and my baby was growing at a normal pace, with a strong heartbeat. I found out I was having a boy.

Everything was going well as I neared the end of my pregnancy. However, a few weeks before my due date, I started feeling a little restless. As my baby got heavier, I became increasingly uncomfortable. I started to feel the need to get the baby out. Not knowing anything was wrong, I couldn't explain why I felt that way. About two weeks from my due date, I felt like my doctor needed to induce me. For about a week, I had contractions that would come and go. I thought it was strange because with Leah, they hadn't gone away but had gotten gradually worse until I delivered. I had not experienced Braxton Hicks contractions with Leah. I don't think to this day that I even know what they are. But I thought maybe that was why I hadn't given birth.

Though my instincts told me I needed to deliver, my OBGYN wouldn't induce me until at least one week before my official due date. I did a lot of walking and ate spicy foods to speed up the process. After a week of mild contractions, I finally headed to the hospital on a Sunday at 3:00 a.m. Once at the hospital, the contractions became more intense. I got an epidural around 5:00 a.m. I wanted to sleep and rest but couldn't because my contractions were so strong. In the birthing room, a nurse came to check the monitors when my baby's heart rate dropped, but by the time she'd checked it, it had already gone back up. Confused, I looked at Jason, but we were told everything was good and didn't press the issue.

As time passed, my contractions got stronger and harder. I told Jason I thought I was going to die. It felt like someone was slamming me in the back. Since we were both unaware of what was really going on, he thought I was exaggerating. Still, he stayed up with me all night and helped me endure the pain and discomfort. Even with the epidural, the pain was still strong. It took everything I had to push the baby out.

Around 10:00 a.m., my substitute OBGYN walked into the birthing room late. My regular OBGYN was also pregnant and due nine days after me but ended up giving birth three days before me. Knowing she might not be able to deliver my baby, she gave me the option of meeting a couple of OBGYNs in advance, but I told her it wasn't necessary as long as someone would be there to take care of me.

By the time the substitute arrived, most of the work was done, or so I thought. Before I knew it, the room erupted in chaos as a team of medical staff rushed in. My son was facing the wrong way. The doctor asked me if she could turn him. I said yes but thought, *What are you talking about? If he is facing the wrong way and needs to be turned, do what you need to do to get him out of me safely.* She turned away to do something, then came back and turned him. Then she told me to push. Within seven minutes from the time she showed up, Jett was born.

When they immediately whisked him away, I thought it was just to clean him up and get his Apgar score. They didn't bring him back to me until I asked if I could see him. His score was frighteningly low. When I did see him, I was in shock. Was this my child? He was so swollen and puffy he looked like a distorted sumo baby. My whole pregnancy, I had no clue there was a single thing wrong. I was confused. I was devastated. I was bawling. I didn't know what to think. I had never felt so helpless.

They wouldn't move me out of the birthing room because my blood pressure was so high they thought I might have preeclampsia. I do not normally have high blood pressure, but it had gone up to 190/90 during the birth. I was surprised, but it all made sense. I had been trying with all my might to push my son out of me because he couldn't help himself. He was overdue, oversized, and had no muscle tone.

Once I was stabilized, they transferred me to an after-delivery room. I briefly wondered why nobody had told me about my elevated blood pressure or recommended another delivery option that wouldn't have put my life in danger, but those thoughts were overshadowed by worry about my son.

Nobody seemed to know what was wrong, but things were clearly wrong. Jett was sent to the neonatal intensive care unit, where they began a series of tests. They tested him for everything from bacteria to diseases, etc., and monitored him in an incubator and set up an EEG. The first physician in charge of the NICU was not helpful. The information we got was inconclusive and scary. In fact, we were so upset after a few days that we filed a complaint about the lack of communication. It must have worked because the next physician on the rotation made sure he answered all our questions.

The first couple of days in the hospital were hard because I didn't have Mom for support as she was in the nursing home. A lot of Jason's family, including my in-laws, were on a trip. My brother came by, but since he had showed up immediately after delivery and we were in shock, we quickly sent him away. Those who did come to visit felt uncomfortable because our mood was so somber. We were assigned a counselor to assist us with our emotions and to answer any questions we had regarding Jett's condition. Between my elevated blood pressure, a lack of sleep, postpartum hormones, and the startling realization that something was really wrong with my son, it was a difficult time.

They didn't inform us about everything they were testing my son for, but I knew that the EEG hooked up to his brain was faulty. The machine showed he was having seizures, but nobody had witnessed a seizure. Luckily, our pediatrician questioned them on it and ordered the hospital to get a new machine. The new machine showed no seizures.

An MRI of Jett's brain showed hypoxia—a deficiency in the amount of oxygen reaching the tissues. The hypoxia was minor, but it was in the area of the brain where the visual cortex lies. They told us it would be fine, but no one could tell us why our son was so unresponsive and lagging behind what was normal for a newborn.

In the NICU, I thought my son looked very odd. At birth, Jett weighed 8 pounds, 13.8 ounces and was 22 inches long. Most of the babies in the NICU had been born prematurely and were much smaller. He was so swollen it was surreal, but it wasn't until about a week after his birth that I realized just how swollen he had been. They measured him and said he was twenty-one inches long. I asked if that was correct since he was born at twenty-two. It's scary to think that he was one inch longer because he was that swollen.

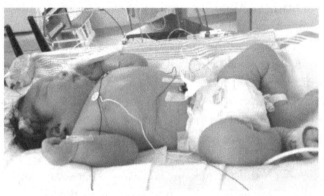

Jett in the neonatal intensive care unit at birth

After roughly seven days, the swelling subsided and Jett began to look normal. We continued to visit him in the NICU and hoped he would be released soon. But more importantly, we wanted the doctors to figure out what was wrong and tell us that everything would be fine. It took eleven days before Jett was able to come home because the hospital had a strict policy about a child gaining weight for a couple of days before being released. Apparently, most children lost weight within the first week before gaining it back. They also wanted to make sure he could drink my breast milk properly.

When I think back to Jett's birth, I remember how difficult it was to process things. From the initial shock of finding out there was something wrong with him, to the challenges of getting him home from the hospital, to the unending questions about everything, there were times I just couldn't process it all. I couldn't figure out what I'd given birth to. Why had he come out that way? There were times where I even felt stupid because I was so confused about everything and devastated because we had no idea what was wrong.

We were physically, mentally, and emotionally exhausted. I was so glad to have Jason with me. His mental and emotional support were invaluable. Whenever I have worries and concerns, he finds ways to keep me calm. He's a solid foundation for our family.

I am a loyal, disciplined person and will keep up traditions or do what I am told if it's for my good or the good of someone else. My family did not have strict traditions for the birth of a child, but Jason's family did. They told me not to leave the house or take the baby out for the first thirty days so I could recover from giving birth and make sure Jett was developing safely before exposing him to all the germs in the world.

With how active I was, staying home for a month seemed like something I would laugh at and never do. Yet, because I believed in honoring family traditions, I complied, except for visiting Jett in the NICU. The other tradition I honored was drinking an after birth tea and eating only chicken soup, pig's feet, and ginger fried rice for the first thirty days. Jason's grandmothers made the pig's feet, my mother-in-law made the chicken soup, and Jason made the ginger fried rice, and I alternated those three meals for breakfast, lunch, and dinner for an entire month.

When I gave birth to Leah, we had a pool at our house. I exercised daily until the morning I delivered, and I wanted to stay in shape after giving birth. I would walk laps around the pool to help with the weight gain and to avoid being sedentary. Miraculously, all the weight I gained from both pregnancies was gone one month after the births because of the diet I followed. I had gained thirty-five pounds with Leah and about forty with Jett. With Leah, I breastfed and pumped successfully, and because I had a whole freezer full, I was able to feed her breast milk long after I weaned her. And breastfeeding did wonders for my metabolism. I was able to eat a lot and was even lighter than before I was pregnant.

I went back to the office and was immediately back in full swing just thirty days after Leah's birth. I just had to figure out when I would feed her or pump each day. Pumping back then was nothing like it is now, and I had to sit strapped to the pump and bottles. Thankfully, as task- and schedule-oriented as I am, I managed to make it work.

Breastfeeding was not as easy with Jett. He latched on decently for the most part, but it didn't seem like I had as much milk. I thought it might be because he was in the NICU for several days and that my milk production was slower, but I breastfed him for ten months. I would have liked to go a full year, but Jett got a few teeth and started biting me. I have to admit I was sad I didn't have the same breastfeeding experience as with Leah, but I didn't dwell on it. And I'm glad I didn't beat myself up over it because I did not know at the time that Jett was having difficulty swallowing. We had no clue what things would be difficult for Jett.

When you imagine bringing a child into this world, you envision a strong, healthy, happy baby. I think sometimes we take the saying "We want a healthy baby" for granted. It was difficult for Jason to watch television programs where people gave birth to normal, healthy children and either didn't want those children or were in an altered state during the process. When you see that happen, you tend to question how life can be so unfair. But sometimes we get things we deserve, and sometimes we get things we don't deserve. There isn't always a logical explanation for the cards we are dealt.

Challenges and Expectations

I used to wonder how people who lost a child during pregnancy, especially if they were very far along, dealt with the loss. I also wondered how people managed giving birth prematurely and spending months at the hospital hoping their child would survive or develop fully and be fine.

Having a baby born premature or with an abnormality is difficult. I applaud the mothers and fathers who must spend the first part of their child's life in the NICU. It's hard to describe the feelings of worry, sadness, disbelief, guilt, and stress you go through while your baby is in the hospital. I can't say it's easier if you know something is wrong with your baby or if you had complications during your pregnancy that prepared you for the possibility of complications during your delivery, but I can say that when throughout your whole pregnancy you have no reason to believe something is wrong with your baby, it's beyond shocking to deliver and find out then.

About four weeks after Jett's birth, we received the genetic-testing results. Jett had a chromosome abnormality. His ninth and nineteenth chromosomes had additions and deletions of genes. One had forty deletions, and both had additions. This odd misarrangement was very uncommon, and we were told there was no one in the world like Jett. While some things were a little obvious, most things were inconclusive. We were given the wait-and-see-what-happens advice. I remember asking the geneticist for more information only to be disappointed. He gave us a print out listing the missing genes, however, he couldn't tell us what each gene represented.

Sometimes we have to trust that things happen for a reason. While I would have liked to have been prepared and to know that my delivery would be rough and that my son would have problems, it was better that it happened the way it did. Although that may sound strange, this is why. When Mom first went into the hospital, I had the required pregnancy quad screening, which came back good. But I never did the amnio test, which doctors recommend you have when you're thirty-five years old, like I was. I never asked my OBGYN why she didn't have me do the amnio test, and she never brought it up. I thought about it, but I was so preoccupied with Mom, I wasn't concerned.

I later found out from the geneticist that we would have known there were issues with my son had we done the amnio. But, to be honest, it could've been detrimental to my health and my baby's health to find out at the time.

I was so worried about Mom I don't think I could have handled any more stress. And I know I would've kept my son regardless. I cannot imagine how many more tests I would have had to endure or what kind of additional worry or concern that would've caused.

Once we knew about Jett's chromosome abnormality, we at least knew why my delivery was so difficult and why Jett looked so strange at birth. But we were still pretty much in the dark about any challenges that lay ahead. There were only a few things we knew at this point, including that Jett had hypotonia, but we didn't know how hypotonia would affect him, and we were still hopeful he would be only slightly delayed.

In those early months, I kept imagining he was just six months behind and that he would eventually reach all his developmental milestones. As he'd hit a certain age, I would compare his development to what a normal child at that age should be able to do and then subtract six months. However, after one year, I realized I should no longer make those comparisons.

It occurred to me that if I kept wishing and hoping for the impossible, I would keep being disappointed. I realized I couldn't put any expectations on Jett other than that I wanted to see some sort of improvement over time. We couldn't put Jett on a schedule and say by this date we expected this to happen and then that to happen. We just made a small goal and focused on it.

Hypotonia is where your muscles are very loose and lack normal strength. As a child, Jett learned to roll from his stomach to his back and vice versa, but he was not able to lift his body using his arms, and so he was never able to crawl and was always lying down. By the time he was three, he could hold himself in a seated position if we propped him up and would stay that way for a couple of seconds. Then he gradually increased how long he could sit up. Eventually, we got him to sit on a stool or a ledge. It was a huge accomplishment. It wasn't until after the age of six that Jett developed the ability to reach for things. He is still learning to hug or to hold on when being carried.

One thing I noticed right away was that he would not focus on anything. When I picked him up, he never looked at me. The connection from his eyes to his brain didn't exist. One of the earliest instinctive forms of communication is where babies visually recognize their parents. It's devastating not to have that connection with your child. You could say it almost felt cold and like he didn't love me because the little things you do to show connection or affection were not there. In fact, it was almost like he did the opposite. It was heartbreaking.

But I loved my son so much, and even though he didn't express love the way a mother hopes, I was determined to express my love for him the same way I would have if he could see and communicate. I made sure I was always hugging him, holding his hand, touching his skin, and telling him how much I loved him.

As time went on, I became deeply concerned about his visual connection. Jett underwent another MRI, as recommended by his neurologist, to see what might be happening with his brain, but this one came back with the same result. Nothing appeared to be wrong other than the small hypoxia where the visual cortex was. Jett's eyes were unresponsive to movement. The eye doctor could not tell us if he had any vision or why he couldn't connect visually with the world around him.

Because the ophthalmologist closest to where we lived couldn't help us, we asked who might be able to, and she referred us to the Casey Eye Institute at the Oregon Health Sciences University. Once we got approved, we scheduled a trip to take Jett for testing when he was eighteen months old.

The eye doctor at the institute gave Jett an electro-retinogram (ERG) test. This test required him to be sedated in order to determine the overall structure of his eyes. Interestingly, the doctor told us Jett's eyes appeared to have normal function overall and that he should be able to see. However, because there was no communication between what his eyes were seeing and his brain, she diagnosed him with cortical blindness. We were disappointed with the news because if the problem had lain with his eyes and not his brain, surgery might have fixed it.

When Jett was younger, he looked up all the time, as if he were looking at the light. Over time, his eyes gradually remained level, and he looks straight now. And yet, despite every effort we've made, his eyes still won't track any type of object or light, although recently, vision specialists have told us he responds best to the color blue.

We know he has vision awareness because he's able to see his sippy cup, even when it's put off to the side, as well as when the spoon is coming to his mouth. We were told that consistency on many different levels could allow Jett to understand an object and therefore achieve a level of visual awareness. Jett also has good instincts as he knows to blink or block something coming at his face, in large part because Jason taught him the cause-and-effect reaction to protect himself.

At mealtime, our routine consisted of feeding him and then giving him milk to drink after. However, he always spit up his milk. Spitting up meant that milk trickled down his mouth and regurgitated in small chunks and larger quantities for sometimes up to an hour after eating. He had this problem even when we burped him, but we didn't know it was a major problem until it was time to go to preschool and we had to instruct his teachers on how to feed him.

We were sent to do a barium-swallow study at the hospital. During the study, Jett was silently aspirating, or swallowing liquids down the wrong pipe without coughing. Most people cough or gag when this happens, but not Jett. It was alarming because liquids could go down the wrong pipe and cause pneumonia, but we found that if Jett ate or drank foods that were of a thicker consistency, there was a lower probability of Jett silently aspirating.

I have been pureeing his food since he was eighteen months old because he never learned to chew properly. Jett is on a somewhat limited diet of oatmeal and strictly pureed foods. This diet keeps him safe, but it's time-consuming for me to prepare. He has not been exposed to a lot of different foods, and we recently had a very bad scare when we discovered he was allergic to peanut butter.

Because Jett had so many other serious issues, we weren't as concerned about his teeth, although we should have been paying more attention. The acid from years of constant throwing up and regurgitation completely ruined his tiny teeth, and by his first dentist visit, they were all decaying. Jett's dentist, a friend of the family, was deeply concerned about the risk of infection.

Jett does not talk. He does not communicate. He does not know how to tell us when something hurts. He can't even point to his mouth to indicate something is wrong. Also, he has a high threshold for pain. The concern was that if one of his twenty rotten teeth became infected and affected another body part, like his heart, we probably wouldn't know until it was too late.

When the dentist told us about his teeth, it scared me. When he discussed the treatment, I was heartbroken. We could put Jett under and remove all his baby teeth, eliminating the risk of infection. That seemed wrong on so many levels. I mean, who could stand to have every single tooth removed from their mouth? How much pain would Jett be in? How uncomfortable would he be afterward? We thought long and hard about the decision. We couldn't ask anyone for advice. I don't even think any of the dentists in that large dental practice had ever removed every single one of someone's teeth. But deep down, we knew we would be eliminating any pain Jett was currently enduring, and we knew we couldn't risk an infection spreading to other areas of his body.

So, for the fifth time, Jett underwent general anesthesia. He had handled it fine the previous times, but there was always risk when you put someone under. Thankfully, the procedure was successful. His gums bled for a day, and he drooled for quite a while after. I wondered how he was supposed to swallow any type of liquid pain reliever, but I learned after the procedure that there's a pain reliever that comes in the form of a suppository. Jett made things much easier for us because he handled everything so well. He is innocent and pure. He is such an angel.

We had no idea how rotten his teeth were until the dentist showed them to us post-surgery. It was alarming to see how brown and decayed they were. I had never seen the full root of a tooth because when teeth fall out, the root is normally not there. But the dentist had to go down to the root of every tooth to extract it, which was not an easy task, especially on a four-year-old. To make light of the situation, we joked that Jett was Toothless, like the dragon in *How to Train Your Dragon*.

The physical wear and tear on the body when you have a child with hypotonia is tough. When Jett was two, Jason had to work weekends due to a schedule change. Caring for Jett by myself all day was rough, especially when I didn't even have relief on weekends. Every time I picked him up, I had to bend down to my knees and then stand up. This included bathing him, changing his diaper or clothes, etc. By the end of his second year, my knees were shot. I had so much pain and swelling I thought I had arthritis but tested for it and was relieved I did not. I had trouble walking down the stairs and could not bend down or squat to my knees. To eliminate the pain, I had to find other ways to do things that did not involve always bending to the ground.

Carrying Jett is difficult because he does not have enough muscle tone to hold himself up or wrap his knees around us to support some of his weight. He easily feels ten to fifteen pounds heavier because of the dead weight. It's like carrying a fifty-pound plus bag of rice. As he continues to grow, we will face other challenges with being able to move him.

At age three, Jett was diagnosed with cerebral palsy. Now it was obvious why he lacked muscle coordination and walking was impossible. Nonetheless, Jason, my mother-in-law, and the school continue to work with Jett to get him to stand and support himself on his own. He was also diagnosed with autism at this time. But other than this diagnosis and support letters from the doctor if we need something, nobody actually provides helpful advice as to how to help Jett. It was frustrating in the early years that the doctors didn't know anything, but as we accepted the unknowns of Jett's unique condition, we shifted toward a team approach in tracking his progress.

I wanted to cry the day I saw a video of Jett attempt to stand with assistance from a seated position on the count of three when he was six years old. Best of all, he had a big smile on his face and seemed proud as everyone clapped and cheered. Jett has been developing the ability to stand for longer periods of time.

Seeing Jett accomplish something so huge yet so simple for the average person makes me appreciate being able to move normally. And while I am thrilled for him, it's bittersweet because of all he is unable to do. He's still not able to walk on his own. If we ever get that to happen, it will be nothing short of a miracle.

For the most part, Jett does not play with toys. For his first Christmas, Santa gave him a stander that looks like a piano. It moves back and forth, the seat spins around, the keys on the bottom make noise when he steps on them, and the top area has piano keys, a spinner, and other things for Jett to play with. For the last eight years, this piano stander has been Jett's best friend, his safe haven, his happy place. It allows him to stand and prop himself up as well as spin around and move back and forth. Since it's built for a nine- to twelve-month-old child, as you can imagine, he's much too big for it. But he finds a way to make it work. We'd love to be able to extend the legs to accommodate his height.

I don't know if Jett will ever be capable of using the bathroom on his own. He wears a size-six diaper, which is the largest traditional size available. I can't imagine very many people having to buy diapers for that long because it is expensive. Fortunately, one of my best clients is a whole-sale distributor of various items, including diapers. I'm not one to ask for favors, but I have gladly asked and will continue to ask for free, damaged diapers.

We suspect that because Jett is blind, he has no idea when it's night or day and, consequently, has never developed a normal sleeping pattern. In fact, as an infant and toddler, he would stay up until two in the morning and rock back and forth in his playpen.

In addition to the rocking as part of self-soothing, Jett has been hitting his face with his fists or pounding his head on the ground while on his stomach for as long as we can remember. His autism explains some of these self-soothing behaviors. On nights he is not super tired and wants attention, he'll start making noise and rocking back and forth the minute he's put in bed and will do so for hours. I have to be careful because the rocking is vigorous and can hurt if he hits me with his arms and legs.

Thankfully, since Jett has had his own bed, while I put him to sleep, I have time to decompress. But it takes a bit of work to get there. I'll climb in bed with him, kiss and hug him over and over, brush his teeth, and give him his medicine. Then I'll write in his school log, read him the short book the school provides, search social media, prepare for the next day, and attend to other tasks. Usually, to help him relax, I have to "smother" him by putting my leg over his chest and trapping his arms so he doesn't hit himself. It's interesting how that soothes some of the children with autism. I'm trying a weighted vest and blanket to see if that makes a difference. It's tricky because it takes awhile for him to fall asleep without interruption. He'll fall asleep for an hour but then wake up shortly after I leave the room. This is why, many mornings, he's super tired and fussy when he gets to school.

You might be surprised to learn that, through it all, Jett is my rock. He keeps me grounded. Life is always throwing me curveballs. There are times when the stress seems unbearable, times I am utterly exhausted, and times I feel like I'm running in circles. There are times I wonder if there's anyone or anything that will ever make my life easier, times I wish all my problems would go away, and times I feel like I need a break from life, or, better yet, a new life. I feel so capable and yet so hopeless. But no matter how bad life gets, at the end of the day, the thing that makes it all worth it is the time I get to spend with Jett.

Mom with Jett in 2015

As parents, we often have expectations for what normal looks like when it comes to our children. If they fall behind or if there is something physical, cognitive, or behaviorally different about them, we feel guilty we did not produce a child who's happy and achieves everything we ever dreamed they would. However, the genetic makeup of a child and the things that happen as they grow are things, more often than not, no parent can control. You can go crazy trying to figure out why something happened, or worrying about whether something could have been done to change things, or about what the future will bring. I've done that at times, and it hasn't led me anywhere except to create undue stress and worry. I've found that the best strategy for finding peace is accepting the children you have for who they are, loving them unconditionally, and having a positive attitude.

Seeing the Stars amid the Darkness

You never dream of having a child who is unable to care for themselves, who will never achieve their independence, and who may never be in a relationship. Instead, you think about feeding them, holding them, changing their diapers, and making sure they are getting enough sleep and are safe. You rejoice as they become more alert each day, look at you as if they know you, react to your voice, smile when you make noises, and make sounds of their own. Rolling over, sitting up, crawling, standing, their first word, and hugging you are milestones to celebrate.

Jason and I went through a period of grieving for the things we would never experience with Jett. But we've learned to let go of those expectations for the most part. The thing that gets me through the sadness of what Jett can't do is to realize that he is not sad because he doesn't know what he's missing. He is happy. The best thing we can do for Jett is to continue to love him unconditionally. If we overthink things too much, it causes undue, undying stress.

Though Jason sometimes feels disappointed that Jett will never play soccer and that they will never have a traditional father-son relationship, he doesn't let that bother him. He focuses on what he can do with Jett. He loves him, supports him, plays with him, feeds him, and helps bathe him and change his diapers. I am so grateful for this, as having a child with special needs can sometimes break a person and challenge a relationship. But we've come to realize what a blessing Jett is to us individually and as a family. His innocence and inability to do anything on his own have given us the opportunity to truly practice unconditional love and selflessness.

As a mother, you want your child to have a normal, happy life. But it's hard to actually define what happiness is. I believe happiness is relative to the person. As we get older, it's sometimes harder to determine what makes you happy and whether you are truly happy. I think about happiness often. I used to think that certain things—like spending time with extended family and doing fun things, like dancing, traveling, shopping, eating, etc.—would make me happy. But as I have gotten older and faced various trials, I've found that when there are things I must do because there's little choice, if I try to focus on the people who make me happy and who I am doing those things for, I am most at peace.

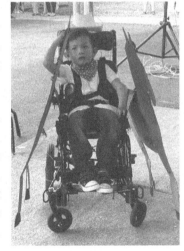

Jett dressed up as a cowboy during his first-grade May Day program

It's difficult to have limitations. We often go through our lives making a big deal out of everything we can't control, and we take for granted what we can. It's not until we lose the ability to do something or are born without it that we truly realize how lucky we are. I have cried over things

Jett will never be able to do. I used to worry about children teasing him or feeling hurt when he didn't respond to them, but kids realize that Jett is special. He has always been one of the most popular kids in school, and everyone knows his name. Amazingly, people love Jett for who he is and do not judge him for what he is not.

I don't know what the future holds. Will Jett eventually be able to walk, talk, or see, to some degree? What kind of care will he need, and what will we be able to manage on our own? I fear the day I cannot carry him myself. There are already days my body aches and my arms tingle from carrying him. And what about the day my in-laws cannot carry him as they assist with his care in the afternoon? Respite care is expensive. This is my reality, but I don't let fear run my life. I pray, hope, and trust that we will be able to manage everything and that it will all work out.

While it's impossible to always be positive, your dominant thoughts affect your mind, body, and spirit. You can choose to nourish yourself with the right thoughts or poison yourself with the wrong thoughts. You can either go downhill and see yourself as a victim or come out stronger and better. Use the hard times to your advantage. It's when the night is the darkest that the stars shine most brightly.

CHAPTER 5

"Every Adversity Has an Equivalent or Greater Benefit"

- Napoleon Hill

Building My Employee-Benefits and Financial-Advising Business

Do you ever look at someone and wonder how they got so lucky? How they became so successful, especially if they didn't have a lot of help? How they came up with a brilliant idea? How their investing turned out so highly profitable? How they found the right spouse? Were they born that talented? It's nice to know there are successful people out there. With the right attitude, we can look at them and be inspired to experience the same success in our lives.

The path to success isn't always what it seems. Often, we don't see the failures experienced along the way; we only see the outcome. But those who have a dream and a desire can do almost anything through perseverance.

In 2011, I got my top securities licenses, settled in with a second firm, and made a transition from selling just supplemental insurance to doing both. My plan was to continue working with the sixty companies I was doing supplemental insurance with and to build my financial-advising practice. The two businesses were similar in that there was some overlap in selling insurance, but the products, sales approach, underwriting process, length of time it took me to get paid for my work, learning and understanding investments, and so many other things were drastically different. I felt like I had gone from one end of the spectrum to the other and that I had two separate businesses fighting for my time.

Since the end of 2011 resulted in a lot of time caring for Mom and early 2012 saw the birth of my son, you could almost say I was destined to fail at being a financial advisor. I was incredibly distracted with my responsibilities on the home front, and yet I had to undertake building another business. I wish I could say I had someone take me under their wing, train me in case scenarios, expose me to their clients, or even share their book of business, but I never had any of that. I built my financial-advising practice entirely on my own.

I didn't get the "normal" training a new advisor would because I was already an experienced producer in another insurance product, did not work at the agency office, had another business taking up my time, and spent a lot of hours taking care of my family. Although my manager was always supportive and made time to help me, a lot of what I did rested in my hands.

I kept plugging away no matter what challenges were thrown my way. I had sacrificed too much to become an advisor. There was no way I was going to fail now. It would have actually been easier to become an advisor back in 2003 when I first looked at it because I didn't have so many things on my plate, but I believe building a supplemental-insurance business along the way helped build my confidence, and the challenges I was facing with my family were only making me stronger.

It was a rocky first couple of years as an advisor, but I was building momentum and growing my client base. I learned monumental lessons about what worked as an advisor versus what worked in the employee-benefits space, and I loved making connections on how the businesses tied in together and understanding how my approach was totally different. What was challenging was branding myself differently. People only knew me as their supplemental-insurance agent. Trying to share how I could help them in many areas was hard to do in a limited amount of time, and I didn't want to just throw out various things I could help with before understanding their concerns and needs.

After much trial and error, I decided I needed to expand on what I could help people with. In addition to helping clients with supplemental insurance and flexible-spending, I partnered with someone selling medical insurance and someone specializing in the best rates for group life, group long-term disability, and temporary disability insurance. I also found carriers I could partner with for long-term care, long-term disability, and life options in the workplace that were similar yet different from the individual advising level. I could also expand and include retirement-plan options and employee-education seminars. With all these opportunities, I just needed a way to let my clients know how I could help them.

In 2014, I opened Inspired Financial Partners, LLC, to bridge the gap and encompass the different ways I could be of service to my clients. The way I do business is, in large part, due to the knowledge and experience I acquired over the years. I dabbled with a few agents, but it was difficult to duplicate my skill level and knowledge. My approach has allowed me to work with clients on many different levels, especially the "middle class," who might not otherwise have access to a financial advisor or the vital information needed to plan, save, protect, and achieve their financial goals.

My original desire to help my family with their financial planning has blossomed into an enterprise that stretches me and keeps me learning. I can say that, more often than not, my head spins at the amount of information I have to keep track of on a daily basis. However, what I have learned over the years is that you are much more capable than you can imagine or will give yourself credit for. Where you are currently at is often far from where you can be.

We tend to shortchange ourselves when it comes to our true potential. We fail to challenge ourselves. There is a side of me that is always scared of change, of failure, and of not being good enough. But I am here to tell you, I have had a lot of success as an advisor, even qualifying for awards and rewards trips throughout the years. There have been more hiccups and rough spots than I would prefer, but I think at the end of the day, it has made me stronger and my business better.

What's your current role in life? Student, employee, business owner, housewife/husband, retiree? Are you happy in that role, or are you just spinning your wheels? If you think you're truly happy, great. But do you want more? Are you capable of doing more to help yourself and others? And if so, what's holding you back? Excuses do not produce results. It's never too late. There will never be a good time, things will never be perfect, and there will always be something going on. If you want to make a change, do it.

As Napoleon Hill says, "Whatever your mind can conceive and believe, it can achieve."

Memories and Moving Forward

Our home is something we often associate with a solid foundation, security, comfort, and happiness. As we all need a place to live, investing in a house and making it a place that fosters fond memories over the years is paramount. We want it to be somewhere we always want to come to and never leave. Many people grow super attached to their homes, especially over time as the memories of their loved ones are often created there. Giving up a longtime home or place of your own is one of the most difficult things you can do.

As 2016 started, I knew there would be a lot of challenges. That included selling Mom's house. Although in the end she was never able to return home following her near-death experience in 2011, we continued to pay thousands of dollars a month to keep the house in case she ever got better. Mom even researched stem-cell therapy to regenerate her nerves and muscles, but it didn't seem like a real possibility. Over the years, I knew we would need to sell the house, but I wanted her to do it when she felt ready because it's sad to think you can never go home.

This process was super emotional not just for Mom, but for me. My family moved into this house in 1986 when I was in fifth grade, and thirty years later, I was saying goodbye to the house I had known most of my life. The fondest memories of my childhood had been made in this home.

When people talk about wanting to stay home as long as possible, I completely understand. However, there may come a point where it is time to let go. Things change, and you cannot always hold on to the past. If we hold on too long, it can negatively affect the present as it prevents us from effectively living life. Given Mom's current physical state, she's actually relieved she does not have to worry about taking care of or paying for the house. Although it's hard to fathom a nursing home as your permanent place of residence, once you require constant care, it's the safest place to be.

I will never forget the fond memories of my past, especially the ones of my childhood with Mom and Dad vibrant and healthy. I wish I could have made many new memories with my parents in my life as an adult, especially now that I have a family. I wish my dad could be here for my kids and witness them growing up. I wish he could be here to joke around with Leah, give her big hugs and kisses, and take her shopping and spoil her.

I'm sad she's missing out on all that. In many ways, I feel like I try to make up for everything my side of the family is not able to provide. I also wish Mom could still do things, like bake her cookies, cook for us, travel with us, be our shopping buddy, and help watch my kids. But now that Leah is getting older and we are close, we share and experience many of the things Mom and I did. I hope Leah will have similar experiences with her kids in the future.

While I had paid for Mom's house for five years after her going into a nursing home, we could only afford to do so as long as her long-term-care policy was able to pay benefits. Once those benefits and her cash were exhausted, we wouldn't be able to pay for the house and her care. As a financial advisor, I felt I needed to understand and make the best decisions for my mom's situation, which in turn would help me advise my clients in the future. Understanding many years in advance what could possibly happen down the road, I started to plan for Mom to live a long life, and that plan included qualifying her for Medicaid.

Qualifying for Medicaid was one of the most stressful things I have ever been through. It took us five years to finally make it work. There was a specific set of rules that had to be followed, and the guidelines were so tricky there were times it felt like I was losing my mind. The pressure, confusion, uncertainty, doubt, and fear were so real. There is no actual handbook on how to do things, and how you get there is based on your unique situation. Because I handled all Mom's finances, it was solely up to me to work with the Medicaid consultants we hired.

There was a bit of relief once I got Mom qualified, but there was still concern and doubt regarding a few loose ends. Nonetheless, I was proud of myself for getting us that far. Part of Mom qualifying for Medicaid meant figuring out what to do with her house. There was a way we could legally transfer the house and still qualify her, and it took a lot of careful and detailed planning, but once it was transferred and Mom qualified for Medicaid, it was time to sell.

I had to take care of Mom's finances before I could take care of my own because her long-term-care policy benefits had run out. We had to tackle step one before we could work on step two, which was selling my house. Moving was a priority for my family at this point because we needed to find a more handicap-accessible house. Although our house had four bedrooms, the only bedroom downstairs was my home office. Moving my office upstairs didn't make sense, and since carrying Jett up and down the stairs was too taxing, he ended up sleeping in a playpen in our living room. Clearly, this was not ideal and could not be sustained long-term.

It wasn't until we put Mom's house on the market that we decided we were ready to sell too. That was in August. Our Realtor wanted us to list our house by October or November at the latest, before the holidays rolled around. We had planned a ten-day trip to Japan in October, so we set a goal of moving out before we left on our trip. That required moving nonessentials into storage and the things we needed to my in-laws while we stayed with them. We were hardly ever home, and selling our home in two months seemed like an impossible task.

What's more, there were things we needed to do before selling. That included repainting the outside of the house and replacing the roof. And we didn't anticipate finding mold under the kitchen sink, caused by a slow leak. Instead of just ripping out the damaged section, we decided to gut the entire kitchen. Luckily, our home-owner's insurance included coverage for mold and I was able to collect the maximum benefit. The new kitchen only cost a couple thousand after the claim money and really improved the value of our home.

Jason played a significant role in the task of moving out before our trip. The kitchen remodel was completed while we were in Japan, and when we came back, the house went on the market. It went into escrow within a couple of days as we immediately had offers. Mom's house went into escrow after a few months on the market, and meanwhile, we also went into escrow on our new house. Needless to say, being in double escrow was quite a roller coaster.

Changing homes can be a difficult and scary process. Change alone implies getting used to something different. You always hope the change is for the better, but when you start the process of looking for a new home, you have no idea if you will find something you want. I sold my childhood home and my first home of seven years in the same week. Embracing the change, understanding the need for it, and focusing on the why helped me through the process. Moving forward and adjusting well works when you have an open mind and a willing attitude.

Peaks of Excitement and Valleys of Despair

Ever look back and wonder how it was possible so many things could happen in just one year? Ever look at those events and experiences and come out grateful, no matter how hard it got? If you haven't experienced any of those years yet, brace yourself, as they will come.

For me, 2016 was one of those years. Between Mom's house repair, a trip to LA for family business, Mom's Medicaid qualification, putting her house on the market, repairing our house and moving out, going to Japan, putting our house on the market, moving in with my in-laws, and Mom having another health scare, there was always something going on.

A local business magazine was taking nominations for an award they gave to forty prominent people in the business community who were under the age of forty. I was aware of the award, knew past winners, and thought it would be such a nice thing to be a part of, though I knew it was a long shot as these awards were not commonly given to insurance agents/financial advisors. However, I thought my accomplishments in the business field, the small areas where I gave back, and my life story might give me a shot. I guess it was enough as I was recognized as a recipient for the award in 2016. I was proud to be included in this esteemed class of successful business leaders.

As mentioned, we moved in with my in-laws while searching for a new home. It was hard not having enough personal space and having to bring a lot of my financial stuff to the office. I was now in the fourth quarter for my employee-benefits business and working hard to qualify for convention on my advisor side. My loan officer kept asking me for the paperwork to start the preloan qualification for our new house, but I kept telling him that I didn't have time.

December was an eventful month. The first week was Jason's birthday, the second I closed on both homes, the third I qualified for convention for the financial advising firm, and the fourth, Mom almost died—again.

With Christmas near, Mom wanted to go shopping for gifts. Our first stop at the mall was lunch at a nice restaurant. She didn't have much of an appetite, so she just ordered stuffed mushrooms. She took five minutes to eat one mushroom and didn't want to eat anymore because her stomach was sore. She also wasn't feeling well and instructed me to tilt her wheelchair back so she was lying down. Needless to say, without any energy, she didn't do much shopping. It was disappointing because we had spent a lot of money for the transport and she was really looking forward to shopping for Christmas presents.

When we got back to the nursing home, she still wasn't feeling well, but I thought she would get better and it would pass. Later that night, though, I got a call from the nursing home saying that Mom needed to go to the hospital. I initially thought she would be released from the hospital, but they ended up keeping her overnight. They wanted to do an endoscopy, but Mom refused to have tubes put down her throat. There was obviously a miscommunication and a lack of cooperation on Mom's part as she eventually left the next day without being treated. In the next few days, her pain worsened, and it became difficult for her to breathe. The nursing home ended up connecting her to a ventilator to provide more oxygen.

When the stomach pain became unbearable, Mom went back to the hospital. We called the ambulance, and I decided to drive to the hospital on my own while a respiratory therapist from the nursing home went with her in the ambulance. At the emergency room, I checked her in, signed the paperwork, and waited for the doctors to tell us what was wrong and what their plan of action was. She was admitted around six o'clock in the evening. I waited in the emergency room for a few hours as they ran their tests and consulted with different team members to decide what to do.

It turned out Mom had sigmoid volvulus—a twisted colon. Given how badly her colon was twisted, along with her ALS (Lou Gehrig's disease) diagnosis in her medical records, the doctors were doubtful she would survive. Surgery was the best option, but they feared she was not strong enough to survive the surgery. An endoscopy was safer, but her colon could rupture in the process, it would be a mess, and they would need to do surgery anyway. There was a lot of back and forth conversation between the ER doctor, his operating team, and me.

Ultimately, I told him, "If you think the surgery is inevitable and necessary, don't complicate it and waste your time on the endoscopy." I could sense he thought Mom would die during the procedure. She was out of it and couldn't make the decision. With my consent as her medical power of attorney, they prepared the team to take her in. I knew I was making the right choice, but I was scared. Crying, I said my goodbyes, feeling like it was the last time I would see her.

Miraculously, she survived. Her strength never ceases to amaze me. The fact that she is still alive has a lot to do with her attitude, grit, and desire to live. It's amazing how her body has not completely given up on her. Around the new year, I got Mom out of the hospital and back into the nursing home, but within a week, she ended up in pain, and we found out she had a bowel obstruction. She was readmitted and stayed another week following an endoscopy to clear the obstruction. In January and February of 2017, we were back at the hospital to treat her bowel obstruction three more times.

The second obstruction was particularly bad. In the emergency room, Mom's systolic blood pressure dropped to fifty. Her blood pressure was drastically affected by her position and tilt of the bed. She looked like she was passing out, and her breathing almost stopped. It was so bad I called my brother and told him to come to the emergency room because I didn't think she would make it. The doctors had to get the tube down her throat to clear her obstruction but couldn't figure out how to do it. They tried for close to an hour as we waited outside the room. Why they couldn't get it down her throat this time around was beyond me. I eventually went into the room and asked them what the problem was. I recommended they give her something to drink and try to put the tube down as she was swallowing and her airway was open. It worked. I think I'd heard Mom say something about it in the past because I somehow knew it would work, but Mom couldn't communicate that to the doctors, and they were unfamiliar with how to help a patient in Mom's condition.

Each time Mom went back to the hospital, I had to drop everything to get her admitted. Each day, I had to go to the hospital to check on her and see if she needed me or someone else to be there. It was always a waiting game in hopes she would get better. I was told the bowel obstructions were from the scar tissue. Without knowing exactly what that meant, I feared this problem would either keep happening or eventually kill her, though I hoped that wouldn't be the case.

Over the years taking care of Mom, I was fortunate to have my husband and in-laws step in to help with my kids. Jason not only made sure I could be there for my mom, he was a great source of knowledge and advice for some of the tough decisions I had to make.

Between my dad, mom, son, and grandpa, I have spent way too much time in hospitals over the last seventeen years. Commuting back and forth to help loved ones has been exhausting. I honestly dread having to go to hospitals as I feel someone's life is often on the line when it happens. Yet I know the person's best chance of survival is there. Isn't it interesting that as we look at the circle of life, we realize that a hospital is often both where you come into this world and where you leave this world behind?

A New Home

Have you ever felt a sense of calm and believed that if something was meant to be, it would happen? It's magical when the stars align and you know something is meant to be. Mom always told me that if you didn't rush or force things, everything would work itself out in the end. I feel this is often true with big decisions, and so I try to never make quick or pressured choices.

Our house of seven years closed the second week of December. We had been viewing homes for sale on a real estate company's website in our desired neighborhood to get a feel for what was out there. We'd chosen this neighborhood because my in-laws lived in it and were an integral part of our kids' lives. Since they were both fortunate to retire from their federal and state jobs at a relatively young age, they enjoy a retirement that consists of babysitting the grandkids and traveling. Having their assistance over the years has been such a blessing.

We physically saw four houses, only one of which we liked. But that didn't motivate me to get my preapproval loan letter with everything else I had going on. Our Realtor inquired about the house we were interested in, and although we had a few reservations about it, we decided it was a good option. After a week or two, we told our Realtor we were interested. He found out someone had put in a cash offer on the house just $20,000 less than the asking price. We were surprised when the sellers rejected that offer because the house had been on the market for a while.

This happened around mid-December. With so many other things on my plate, there was no time for my loan paperwork. I had to get through two escrows, qualifying for convention, Mom's life-threatening hospitalization, and wrapping up year-end business before I could start working on the loan.

On Friday, December 30, I was ready. The following Monday, January 2, 2017, my preapproval loan letter was ready. We sent it to the Realtor, who submitted our offer on January 4. By January 5, we were in escrow. It's pretty remarkable that we only looked at four houses because we'd originally thought it would be an impossible feat to find what we needed. Yet we found a house that was beyond what we thought we could get. The house was perfect and seemed to be waiting until we were ready.

What confirmed this belief was our closing date. We were supposed to close on February 20. As I was preoccupied with Mom being in and out of the hospital in January and February, we were fortunate that the loan process went smoothly. About a week prior to our closing date, our loan officer called and asked if we wanted to close early. I was excited and said, "Yes, when can we close?" Before he answered, I knew he would say February 17. I immediately called Jason to share the good news. When I asked him to guess the date of the closing, he already knew.

While February 17 may seem like any other day, it has had a lot of meaning for me. It was my parents' wedding anniversary, my childhood best friend's birthday, and the day my father passed away. Every February, it seemed as if I would lose it just a little. The anniversary of my father's passing had been difficult for me for years. When our house miracle took place on that date, it felt like my father had played a role in helping to turn a sad day into a happy one. Of all of the days in a year, our new house had somehow landed in our hands on a day of significance.

I thought 2017 was going to be smooth sailing after Mom's hospital stays and moving into our new home. However, in April and May of that year, Mom was kicked off Medicaid. Without disclosing too much of what I went through, I'll just say that selling the house put her in jeopardy and that it took close to two months to prove that her qualification was fully justified. I'll never forget the additional stress I went through knowing that an unjust qualification could result in a year of back payments, and enormous penalties, and make it impossible for Mom to qualify again in her lifetime. Despite stress that I think is too much for a child to bear, I'm glad it was taken care of and the qualification was legal and warranted according to the rules. After the records were set straight, I could sleep at night.

Selling Mom's home and moving my family was a huge undertaking. While there were times things seemed to fall right into place, there were times things were nerve-racking. There were periods of great uncertainty, fear, and anxiety during the process, and I had to learn to control my thoughts and emotions. It helped to visualize my end goal and work my way back to the present to mentally prepare for what was going to transpire. It also helped to plan and prepare as best I could and to understand that the bumps and challenges that arose were only temporary setbacks. I knew that having the right attitude throughout the process could impact not only the outcome but what happened along the way.

CHAPTER 6

The Hits Keep Coming

Growing Pains

When a new year begins, we look forward to starting all over again and are hopeful the new year will be better than the last. We make resolutions and set goals. I create a long list of personal and business goals every year. I get excited for change and a better year and let the past be the past. I've found that if you set goals to accomplish things, it brings a renewed sense of energy and excitement.

The first day of 2018 started with a bang, literally, when on New Year's Eve fireworks exploded in Leah's face. Setting off fireworks on New Year's Eve is a big tradition in Hawaii. Children are exposed to the different types of fireworks from a very young age based on what's age-appropriate and safe. We had boxes of a new firecracker that came individually packed in sawdust. These single red firecrackers, called Torpedoes, were slightly larger and more powerful than the small white Pop Pops young children played with. Leah was tasked with separating the torpedoes from the package and put them in a container to make them easy to grab and throw.

All of a sudden, there was a big boom and loud crying. When Jason and I first got to Leah, she was hunched over with her eyes glued shut. She was crying hysterically and had cuts, saw dust, rocks, and red firework paper all over her hair and body. We quickly got some water and wiped down her face, then tried to wash out her eyes, but they were so sore she could barely open them. We had to pry them open to get the dust and debris out. What I took out was scary. She could not hold her eyes open on her own, couldn't see, and was in a lot of pain. Also, the noise from the explosion had made her ears sensitive, and she was panicking from noise and people talking. It crossed my mind that this explosion could make her blind. I prayed that wouldn't happen. I mean, what were the odds that I could have two blind children? I was so scared.

Fortunately, my eye doctor was one of my clients, and we had a relationship where I could reach out to her on New Year's Eve. I felt much better after speaking with her. She provided advice and guidance for that night, and we were able to get Leah examined at her office on New Year's Day. It seemed like an eternity as we waited to have her eyes checked when, in actuality, it was within twenty-four hours. Thankfully, the scratches on Leah's eyes healed after a couple of weeks. At seeing the cuts on her leg, the doctor said Leah could have easily lost her sight had she not closed her eyes as fast as she did when the explosion happened.

I wondered if I would ever catch a break when Jett and I ended up getting sick shortly after the incident with Leah. We didn't recover until mid-January. It was a rough start to the year. Despite Mom being in and out of the hospital the first few months of 2017, it had been a great year. We'd moved into our beautiful home, and Leah had started middle school at my high school alma mater. Now that life was a little more settled, I wasn't consumed with everyone else's problems. I wouldn't say that my life was simple or normal, but, rather, as simple and as normal as my life could get.

I started 2018 with high goals, but within a month or so, those goals were a moot point. I fell into a rut. I had two large additional expenses—the cost of our new home and Leah's tuition—on top of the many existing expenses. I had depleted a lot of my savings fixing up and furnishing the house. Then one of the lines of business I had done well selling the two years prior changed its compensation structure, basically cutting my commission in half.

For the first time in fifteen years of building my career and businesses, I was burned out. I was unmotivated, distracted, and unhappy. I was stressed about how I was going to earn the income I needed to support my family, my business, and personal expenses. As I wasn't paid a salary by anyone, I needed to make sure I always had enough to pay the bills, yet I didn't always get paid quickly for what I sold. Thus, cash flow could be a big problem if I wasn't earning surplus amounts of commission.

I would come to work without any real focus and would often fall asleep at my desk at random times during the day. Maybe you could argue I was somewhat depressed. I know that when I was depressed after my dad died, I was always tired.

As the year progressed, I was having an increasingly hard time managing the pressure of maintaining a certain income. I was so burned out and off track I knew something needed to give, but I didn't know what. I gave myself the year to figure it out. Motivation was never something I'd lacked. In addition to a mind that required constant growth and challenge, I had a strong inner drive. And while I was hard on myself, I was also very understanding. I knew I had to give myself time to work through my feelings.

Many times in my life I have found myself in not-so-ideal situations. When these things first happen, I tend to be very emotional, but once I take the time to analyze what's happening and evaluate my feelings, I give myself permission to be upset, hurt, sad, or whatever those initial feelings may be. After that, I look at the situation and see if there's anything I can do to change it. If it's something beyond my control, I learn to accept it. Then I seek to deal with it and figure out how to find a more positive perspective on the situation.

If I hold on to any anger or the feeling of being on the short end of the stick, it makes my attitude more negative. And once my attitude turns negative, it becomes difficult to put on a happy face and focus on things other than myself. It's hard to function at a high level when you focus only on your problems and feel like it's "woe is me" all the time.

While it was sometimes therapeutic to share my burdens with others, other times, I felt like it was too much information. While most people were sympathetic, I didn't want to feel like I was unloading my problems on them. It wasn't just with what I said, though, it was my overall attitude. I knew that if I was feeling sorry for myself and down all the time, I couldn't effectively help others.

As the year progressed, I sensed a change coming. I traditionally liked consistency and routine. I was not a fly-by-the-seat-of-my-pants type person. I understood there were many benefits to change, but I had been through every huge change imaginable over the last seventeen years. Change can be very stressful and often requires a lot of work and then a lot of adjustment, but I believe change is necessary. If it's a change for the right reason, it often leads to bigger and better things once you allow yourself to accept it.

I wouldn't say I'm fast-acting when it comes to change for myself. When it is for myself, I evaluate things differently and have more emotional involvement than when I am preparing for change that impacts others more than me or just as much as me. Because I am empathetic, I think about how a change I make might impact others in every aspect possible. If it will negatively impact others, this will often change my decision, no matter how good the change may be for me.

Taking other people's feelings into consideration often leads me to a stalemate because most of the time, change affects everyone, both positively and negatively. Sometimes I wish I would focus on only how a change will impact me. But I suppose at the end of the day, when you truly consider how you will impact others, you feel much better about your decisions.

Have you ever heard that the definition of insanity is doing the same thing over and over again and expecting a different result? When what we are doing changes beyond our control, we must change as well. Recently, I hit a large bump in the road with my business, as many do at some point. Finding ways to overcome the obstacles I'm faced with is much easier said than done. Pulling myself out of the rut took a lot longer than expected. In the last two years, I have made a lot of changes to my business on all levels. Every day, there are new businesses opening and old businesses closing. Those businesses that can continue to survive and thrive must continually adapt to the changes around them and ignite internal changes from within.

The Opportunity of a Lifetime

When opportunity is presented, do you take it? If something falls in your lap that you didn't seek, do you consider it or stay the course? I think it's different for everyone because I know a lot of people who frequently change jobs or seek new adventures. They are always looking for the next greatest thing and seemingly thrive on the excitement change brings with it. There are also many who are content with where they're at, who like consistency, and who are not sure change is positive.

I'm frequently approached by other companies wanting me to join their agencies or open up a franchise office. With how complicated my life and two businesses already are, I usually nip these conversations in the bud. However, knowing changes needed to be made in my life, I was more open to a conversation.

When a headhunter representing another financial-advising company reached out to me, I was interested because the company was one I had spoken with in the past and considered working for. And I knew the local recruiter, who was still in the same position from many years prior. We went back and forth several months before I decided to consider working with them depending on who I would work with. At the end of the day, I was offered "the opportunity of a lifetime," as they put it—to work with the company's most successful local team. It was supposed to have been a win-win for everyone.

A lot of people say that moving is one of the bigger stresses in life. Changing jobs or companies comes close. In order to accept this opportunity with the new financial-advising firm, I need to move out of my office and into theirs. It was a task to clear out fifteen years of files, paperwork, and furniture. I cried almost every day for the twenty-eight days before the move was official, sad to leave a company where I felt so at home and where I loved the people.

While it seemed like a good thing, I was also closing the door on having my own business office, and I knew what that had represented to me all these years. My business had been built, controlled, and dictated by what I sold and how I helped my clients. I was my own boss and in complete control of every decision made, and being my own boss allowed me to manage the many personal challenges I had over the years without having to answer to anyone or feel guilty. I could manage my time as needed and focus on what was important when it was important.

This huge business move meant closing a door on one chapter in my life. I had to believe that changing directions did not mean failure. Sometimes we do what we do only because we have to. We figure we've been given what we're given, and if it isn't broke, we don't need to fix it. Sometimes I make excuses to hide in my comfort zone and say that everything will be okay because I don't want to change.

But I have to ask myself who I am hurting by not being willing to change. And if I keep doing what I am doing, how will that impact me in the long run? Do you get excited about making changes only to doubt whether you can actually make those changes? It can be difficult to determine ahead of time if the change is actually for the better, if you're just scared, or are making excuses because you either lack the confidence or desire. Without experience, we often make assumptions about whether something is good or not, but we won't know until we try.

We always hear that when one door closes, another one opens. That's a positive spin on a negative situation in which you don't have a choice on a matter that has changed. It's interesting to be on the opposite end, where you initiate a change on something that hasn't limited you. In February 2019, I chose to close one door and open another. While sometimes it would seem a no-brainer to seek something better, the older we get and the more complicated our lives are, the harder that is to do. With blind faith, I made a change that should have provided me a better opportunity.

Should have. Once I got there, my gut told me it wasn't right. While on the outside something can look so good, you can't really know if it's what you want until you're on the inside. There was a lot of good that came with the opportunity, but it just wasn't the right fit. I tried to convince myself it was just adjusting to the change that was making me uncomfortable and unhappy, and I tried to move forward and embrace the new company, my new team, my new surroundings, and the new systems. But as the days passed, I started feeling more trapped and more miserable. It seemed I was committed and unable to turn back.

A couple of months later, I decided to go back to my old company. It took courage to admit my mistake. Nobody likes feeling like they made the wrong choice or feel they've wasted their time and the time of those around them. I had never put myself in a position where there was so much on the line, so much at stake. But the older I get and the more I have on my plate, I realize I have to be happy with my work. It's something that, ultimately, I can control and that doesn't directly impact my loved ones.

I've asked myself why I made the decision to move in the first place, and why, if it was that big of a decision, I didn't do more due diligence. I've learned that sometimes when we are presented something that seems to align with the things we desire, we simply hope we can make it work without really looking at the details.

A lot of times, I'm afraid to ask for help or to ask the tougher questions. And sometimes, to avoid confrontation, I'm not as direct as I should be. I guess you could say that's why I never liked having multiple offers to choose from. Along the same lines, I don't like letting people down.

Thankfully, my former manager and general agent welcomed me back with open arms. They couldn't believe I'd made the move in the first place. I thought the transition to my old company would be an easy one. However, starting over with contracts, licensing, background checks, fingerprinting, and setup proved to be a long and difficult process. I went from working in my business office to the new company's office, back to my home office for a couple of months, and then to my old firm's agency office.

I'd felt like 2019 was destined to be a year of lucrative changes, but it proved to bring more challenges and setbacks than I had experienced in my career up to that point. As I always try and look for the positive, I searched for lessons learned and reassurance in myself. I learned that what others may think is an opportunity of a lifetime may not be my opportunity of a lifetime. I learned I need to be in control of my time and what I do and that I cannot be too restricted by any one company or team. I learned that while there may be better ways to make money, I need to get there on my own terms and make sure it fits my business model. I learned that what I do is worthwhile because it allows me to help everyone, not just the wealthy. And I learned that I'm good at what I do and am not less valuable than other advisors in my field just because my specialties are different from theirs. This helped me tremendously because I'd always admired other advisors and felt they were better than I was. To have been chosen to work with the best of the best, I knew I was good enough. I have a deep respect for my colleagues and what they do, but I no longer feel inadequate. The change empowered me to be proud of what I do.

I dream that, one day, work will be easy and money will just come to me. Meanwhile, I know there's no escape to the hard work and discipline required to get there. There are no shortcuts to true long-term success. With the transition back to my old company, I had to decide how I wanted to run my business and spend my time. It was almost like starting new, although I wasn't really. But having a new attitude and perspective is what got me out of my rut and what's inspiring me to make my business even better. 2020 represents a new year, new goals, and a new vision. As 20/20 is synonymous with vision, my word for this year is *focus*. I'm going to focus on what I want with a can-do attitude and a refreshed spirit to meet my goals.

CHAPTER 7

It's a Wonderful Life

Life is truly an eventful journey. I never thought I would be an author when I was younger. Since I'd always struggled in English, I doubted myself during this whole process of writing and feared people would find my book boring, my story inconsequential. The courage to get started, to keep going, and to believe in myself came because others believed in me. I couldn't have done it alone and wouldn't have done it if I didn't truly believe my story could help others.

Though I would not want to relive the last seventeen years, I am deeply grateful for what I've learned: You start each day afresh and anew despite what comes your way. You set goals you want to accomplish. You move forward and learn from the past, not dwelling too much on it. It's a constant battle to stay positive and live life with hope in the midst of trials, but the hope that things can always get better is what keeps us going. And in the process of moving forward one step at a time, we eventually find that life can be wonderful in spite of the storms—and maybe because of them.

I have been through so many extreme changes in my life. In fact, I have been through so many you would think I welcome change. But that is far from the truth. I like routine, I like safety, I like knowing what I know. I don't like unknowns, I don't want to fail, I'm scared of what true success will bring, and if I achieve true success, I am afraid of losing it as I have had such a challenging life. When it comes time to make changes, especially for myself, I can be slow-moving.

But change is inevitable, so the more welcoming and accepting you can be to change, the more successful you will be in adjusting to it. I realize now how unpredictable life really is. Many days we think we have everything all planned out and are making the right decisions for our future. Sometimes we can see things coming or successfully predict the outcome of a course of action. Other times we have no idea what's about to transpire until it does and we are looking back on it.

We are all faced with decisions—from decisions about what we will wear or eat, to what kind of car to buy, to decisions that involve work, relationships, and family. But the most important decision we can make is choosing what our attitude toward ourselves and life will be. We can choose to be happy, to have hope, to help others, to always improve and achieve our goals, to be healthy, and to plan for future success. And while we may not have much control over the challenges life presents us with, we have full control over how we will respond to our circumstances.

Mom has lost her independence, and while many would consider her life tragic, depressing, and not worth living, she doesn't see it that way. She has chosen to be grateful for the life she has, and because of that decision, she is happy in spite of her struggles. She has truly discovered the secret of happiness. Jett was born without the ability to see, talk, walk, or communicate. He's 100 percent dependent on those around him and isn't able to enjoy life experiences that most of us take for granted. He can't see all the beautiful things in the world, he can't talk with a friend or enjoy a slice of pizza. He can't play soccer or swim. And yet he can smile and when he does, it lights up the room. His sweet personality is infectious and is a blessing to those around him. In his own way, he chooses to bear his own struggles patiently.

Husband and children at a wedding in 2019

You could say their life is terrible, but it's all a matter of perspective. When things go south, I remember what Mom told me on that day long-ago as I cried when I realized what my son's special needs could mean for us. She said, "It is what it is." She told me that if I couldn't change it to not lose sleep over it and to accept it and move on. Since that day, I've learned there is great power in her advice. When we decide to move forward in spite of our problems, we begin to create our own hopeful future. We find strength and courage to turn our stumbling blocks into stepping stones. And we learn to create a successful, happy, wonderful life, no matter what heartache, calamity, or disaster the universe has placed in our path.

I hope you've found a way to relate my story to your life, and I hope the connections you have made give you perspective, inspiration, and motivation. Remember that when life gets difficult, as it inevitably will for each of us, we need to deal with it, accept it, and move on.

It's okay to feel sorry for yourself once in a while or wonder what you did to deserve this. That's only human. However, the best way to get out of any slump is to think about what you can learn from it, see if there is anything you can do to make it better; take action instead of allowing depression, insecurity, or fear of failure keep you stuck in a rut; and hold on to a hope that things will get better. Sooner or later, they always do. Most importantly, you must believe you have the strength to get through anything and everything and that nothing in your life can hold you back unless you let it. When things get difficult, use hope to inspire strength.

Note to the Reader

Thank you so much for taking the time to read my book. I hope you have found inspiration and insight for your life. I would appreciate it if you could help leave a review on Amazon and Goodreads. In addition, please share my story with your friends and family who may be impacted by reading it.

If you would like to contact me, please e-mail me at lianekchong@gmail.com.

Follow me on my Facebook Business Page, Liane K. Chong. I share daily inspiration and motivation on my Instagram group, @lianekchong.author, and on my Facebook Group, Liane Inspires. You can also find more information on my website, lianekchong.com.

About the Author

Liane was born and raised in Honolulu, Hawaii. She received her BA in business management from the University of Puget Sound in Tacoma, Washington, and lived in Portland, Oregon, before moving back to Hawaii to build her career. She is a self-employed business owner and financial advisor for a major company, as well as an employee-benefits specialist. She has won several awards and rewards trips over the years and was also recognized by a major local magazine for being a Top 40 under 40 recipient in 2016.

She is married and a mother of two children—a teenage daughter and a son in elementary school who was born with a rare chromosome abnormality. He has multiple special needs that include cortical blindness, hypotonia, cerebral palsy, autism, and he cannot walk or talk. In addition to taking care of her children, Liane has been a caregiver for her physically incapacitated mother since 2008.

Liane loves her work helping families better plan and prepare for their future. Outside of work, she enjoys spending time with her family, dancing, volunteering for her high school, helping with the family Chinese lion dance club, and traveling.